An Unwanted Child

Wanted By GOD

An Unwanted Child

Wanted by God

Gwen Lawan Johnson

Belleville, Ontario, Canada

Wanted By God

Copyright © 2001, Gwen Lawan Johnson

ISBN: 1-55306-283-3

For more information or additional copies, you may contact:

Gwen Lawan Johnson
3475 Sevilla Drive
Soquel, CA 95073 USA

or for review:

Amazon.com

Guardian books is an imprint of *Essence Publishing,* a Christian Book Publisher dedicated to furthering the work of Christ through the written word. For more information, contact: 44 Moira Street West, Belleville, Ontario, Canada K8P 1S3.
Phone: 1-800-238-6376. Fax: (613) 962-3055.
E-mail: info@essencegroup.com
Internet: www.essencegroup.com

Printed in Canada
by

Dedicated to
the memory of my beloved husband,

Kerry

who taught me the meaning of
unconditional love.

Love always protects, always trusts, always hopes,
always perseveres. Love never fails
(1 Corinthians 13:7-8).

and

To the members of the Comfort Through Christ Group
at the Twin Lakes Church in Aptos, California. I am
indebted to all of you in this amazing group who daily
live with pain. You have been an inspiration to me and a
joy to fellowship with weekly. I love each of you and
cherish our time together.

I didn't want to put this book down. It was like listening to a friend share her innermost being, spirit to spirit. As each page unfolded, I felt the words of God coming alive and a deep connection to the author's spiritual awakenings and growth. *Wanted by God* is rich and encouraging with great Scripture passages interwoven throughout.

Erin M. Kelly
Associate Editor
Massage Magazine
Santa Cruz, California

Wanted by God, is a powerful statement of God's enduring love reflected through the life of Gwen Johnson. She was unwanted by her parents, mistreated, and suffered numerous physical and emotional problems. Gwen had times of terror, dread, and rejection, but through it all she demonstrated the faithfulness of God who loved her and restored her self-esteem. The reader will be captivated by Gwen's openness as she surveys her life's journey and reinforces the lessons she has learned with appropriate Scripture.

Dr. Bryce Jessup, President
San Jose Christian College
San Jose, California

Gwen Johnson's story is fascinating for anyone, and particularly for those who struggle with physical or emotional pain. Gwen can fully empathize, as this one woman has recovered from trauma as diverse as divorce, widowhood, severe illness, and disability. That she has done so with such triumph and optimism is a testimony to the work of Christ in her heart.

Pastor René Schlaepfer
Twin Lakes Church
Aptos, California

Table of Contents

Acknowledgements

My profound thanks to Gloria Graham for giving me the push I needed to start writing by introducing me to a critique group after I told her God was calling me to write.

Sitting next to JoAnn Wendt one day in Bible Class, I heard she was a writer.

I asked for her help. Through JoAnn I learned the basic steps to start me on the path of writing, and under her I became a published writer. JoAnn moved to Reno, Nevada.

Then God brought Lousie Vernon into my life. Louise has been my mentor, friend, and instructor, helping me cut down on my overabundance of words and to sharpen my writing skills. She is seriously ill at present and extremely missed.

My love and praise go to the Holy Spirit who taught me the Word of God, gifting me with a strong faith and shaping my concept of my heavenly Father, and my Savior, Jesus Christ; and making me aware of how He gave me His strength to become bold in talking to others about my faith in God, ever since I was a child.

I owe a tremendous amount to Pastor Albert Jesse who taught me during my confirmation years. He was pastor of St. Paul's Lutheran Church in St. Joseph, Missouri, and later became one of the Vice Presidents of the Missouri Synod.

I thank Rev. Marvin Rickard, through whom my beloved Kerry came to a well-grounded understanding of the Word, and who for years brought messages that inspired me along with thousands of others, at the Los Gatos Christian Church in Los Gatos, CA.

My thanks to Pastor Carl Palmer through whose teaching on Sunday morning in Bible Class, I learned to trust God in all things. Carl's statement that Jesus lived the only life acceptable to God, caused my prayers for Jesus to come live His life in and through me, changing me to become a person

I could respect. Carl was then a pastor, at the Los Gatos Christian Church in Los Gatos, CA.

Pastor René Schlaepfer, Twin Lakes Church, Aptos, California, where I currently attend, is the most fascinating communicator of the Word I have ever had the privilege of hearing. His messages fill me with the assurance of God's love and His grace and help me appreciate the great sacrifice Jesus made on my behalf. They let me know that, too, the power of God's Holy Spirit is always at work making all believers into the people God wants us to be.

Without Michael Rumph, my next-door-neighbor from San Jose, traveling to Soquel to help me get all of my stories lined up from a variety of places in my computer into one file, I would never have been able to turn them into book form.

And, without Steve, my next-door-neighbor in Soquel, coming to my aid when my computer and printer malfunctioned, and finally putting the entire book in disk form to send to the publisher, it could never have been published.

Thanks to each of you for the part you played in helping me to write the book and for helping me get it ready for publication.

Introduction

Through true stories told over nearly seventy years of my journey with God, I show how learning to listen to God and trusting Him completely through trials and suffering brought me into a deep, personal relationship with Jesus, while He filled my life with experiences far beyond the desires of my heart and blessed me with His love, peace, and joy.

If you are someone who believes you don't deserve God's love, I was just like that. Then one evening I was reading the first chapter of John, which had always been one of my favorite chapters in the Bible, when the words from the 12th and 13th verses leaped from the page and imprinted themselves on my heart and mind.

Yet to all who received him, to those who believed in his [Jesus] *name, he gave the right to become children of God—children born not of natural descent, nor of human decision or a husband's will, but born of God* (John 1:12-13).

God was telling me that I had been born because He wanted me.

Wanted by God! That thought pulsated over and over in my brain. It no longer mattered that my mother had not wanted me. I wasn't just a mistake after all, because God wanted me to be His child. During this particular reading, God's Holy Spirit interpreted this passage for me: *"You have been born again of God. You are His child and an heir of His heavenly Kingdom."* I knew these words were true.

This promise that I had been born anew as God's child was not just for me, but God wants all people to acknowledge their belief in Him and receive Jesus as their Savior from sin, allowing Him to become Lord over their lives and be born again.

By making Jesus, Lord, instead of our power being taken away from us, God gives us His supernatural power to get things accomplished. We gain new freedom because we are no longer enslaved by sin which weighed us down and kept us from becoming all we could be. Seeking to obey God puts our lives in harmony not only with God, but with all those with whom we come into contact.

God looks down from heaven on the sons of men to see if there are any who understand, any who seek God (Psalm 53:2).

The Bible also states: *The lions may grow weak and hungry, but those who seek the Lord lack no good thing* (Psalm 34:10).

I can attest to that. I have been seeking to know God better since I was a child. However, in my fondest dreams I could not have imagined the incredible mate God sent into my life or the marvelous travels throughout the United States and the world He provided for us to enjoy, together. Nor had I ever considered being a writer. These were all gifts from our awesome God.

Although the first part of my life was filled with pain, trials, and losses, I now know God was preparing me for the wonderful future He had planned for me. And I am convinced that the life that lies ahead of this one is even more desirable.

Before gathering these seventy-two true stories from my life, I recalled how Jesus spoke to people in parables. He used simple narratives, speaking of earthly things, but each story contained a deeper spiritual meaning. God has been speaking to me all through my life, through His Living Word, which is as active and alive today as it was in Bible times.

God breathed His Living Word, the Bible, into being, making it relevant for all mankind. It is God's Living Word breathed from His divine impulse to our hearts and minds if we will only listen and believe.

God loves us because He created us and He desires fellowship with each of His children. He takes great pleasure in what we accomplish and loves it when we come to Him to seek His advice and talk things over with Him, and ask Him to show us what is best for our lives. He wants our love and our praise for this wonderful world He has created for us, and He loves to hear us tell Him we love Him.

God has given us so much and yet we spend so little time appreciating Him. He wants to talk to us and He hopes we will listen to His advice because it pleases Him and brings us joy.

His voice may become commonplace, uninteresting, or even lost to us, because of our preoccupation with the things of this world. Possessions, belongings, our hunger for the "better" things in life, pull us away from spending quiet time with God, focusing on His Word and His will for our lives. I knew God revealed Himself through His Word, but I had never known His still small voice until one day in my late thirties, when He was trying to communicate with me but I refused to listen. I have relayed this lamentable incident in this book and I tell how I learned to listen for God's voice.

My hope is that God's Holy Spirit, who delights in revealing the things of Christ to us, will make His voice known to those who read this book.

My desire for all who read *Wanted by God* is that each of you may hear, feel, and experience Jesus at work in your own life and not give up when life grows difficult or painful; but continue to seek a deeper relationship with God and find the joy of living an exciting and abundant life through Christ Jesus our Lord.

Gwen Lawan Johnson
Soquel, California

1
Learning to Call on the Lord

I cry with my voice to the Lord. Before him I tell my trouble (based on Psalm 142:1-2).

🌼 Born Wanting Love

🌼 Light Blindness

🌼 Pleasing God Brings Love, Peace, and Joy

🌼 A Key to Wisdom

🌼 Maturing in the Word

🌼 An Extraordinary Gift from God

🌼 Moments of Terror

I pray... he may strengthen you with power through his Spirit in your inner being, so that Christ may dwell in your hearts through faith (Ephesians 3:16-17).

🏵 Born Wanting Love

I was an unwanted child.

My mother often told me, "Another baby was the last thing we wanted when you were born!" I made my appearance in 1929 when our country was reeling from the shock of the big depression. My father's job was wiped out, savings were lost, and my little brother Henry was not yet two.

One thing my parents didn't need was another mouth to feed. However, listening to my mother repeating this statement over and over, I began feeling guilty for having been born.

Although I never considered myself an abused child, by today's standards I was not only unwanted but abused, as well. My dad turned me over his knee, doubled his wide exercise strap in two and gave me some very hard beatings. Growing older, I hated dressing down for gym because it made my friends sick to see the black and blue bruises spreading from my buttocks to the back of my knees.

I never blamed Dad for the whippings because he was following Mother's demands. Mother insisted I needed a spanking for something bad I'd done or for not doing something she'd asked me to do. I tried to tell her I hadn't heard her ask me but it never did any good. If Dad had been present during the time my mother became angry at me, I think he would have defended me and I doubt that he would have spanked me.

Trying to prevent such painful strapping, one day I took our big garden scissors and cut my daddy's four inch wide, hard, red rubber exercise strap in two. I buried one half in a hole in the backyard and one half in the front yard in the deepest hole I could dig. Dad wondered where his exercise strap was, but he couldn't find it anywhere.

Years later, Dad dug up one half of his exercise strap, but he couldn't figure out how it had gotten buried in the backyard. "I always wondered what had happened to this good exercise strap and here it is, well, half of it anyway," he said holding up the strap. I certainly didn't intend to make any explanations. I held my breath afraid he'd figure out what I'd done.

One day, Miss Harriet, my elocution teacher, told my Mom, "I don't think Gwennie hears us when we speak to her unless we're close enough she can watch our lips to see what we're saying."

My mother had placed me in this class to help me pronounce my "r's" correctly. I made the letter "r" sound like a "w." Miss Harriet taught a type of public speaking to a group of private students, showing us how to recite entertaining readings in a loud, memorable way. We learned how to speak with expression so the audience could hear and understand clearly what was being said. I learned to stand in front of large groups of people and recite readings. The first one I recall was, "I have ribbons on my shoulders and bows on my feet. I'm my daddy's darling; don't you think I'm sweet?" At that time I was only five.

Some of the older children would carry on conversations with other people, changing their voices to depict different characters. Miss Harriet was a very capable teacher and her students were popular with the groups of people who heard them. One of the older girls traveled and presented readings in competition. She entered contests where the art of elocution was judged for the clarity of the words and the expression used.

Miss Harriet would take her group of pupils to the old folks' homes, churches, and even to the insane asylum, to entertain the people there. I looked at all those strange, wild and angry-looking faces at the asylum, and became so flustered I walked right past the microphone and went to the middle of the stage to start my recitation.

After Miss Harriet told my mother that I couldn't hear when she turned her back and spoke to me, my mother remembered my insisting I hadn't heard her when she asked me to do certain chores. She recalled she'd been angry because I didn't do what she'd asked. Now her question was, had I heard her or was I faking it?

Mother devised a way to determine whether or not I could hear. Knowing how much I loved ice cream she waited until her back was turned away from me and asked, "Gwennie, do you want an ice cream cone?" I didn't answer. Then she turned and faced me and asked the same question.

I answered immediately, "Sure I want an ice cream cone. Do you mean right now?"

Finally, my mother agreed that what Miss Harriet had said was true. She was convinced I'd lost most of my hearing. I heard what people said when they were facing me and I could read their lips. I had learned to lip read without knowing it.

When I started school, my mother requested that I sit at the desk in front of my teacher. It worked until my teacher turned her back and spoke while facing the blackboard.

Gwen Lawan Johnson

My mother took me to the doctor to see what had caused my hearing loss. He said both of my eardrums were ruptured from abscesses or bad ear infections, that had caused my eardrums to break. The doctor said until my eardrums healed again, I would continue to have hearing problems.

The first night of ear pain that I can remember, happened when I was four. I ran into my parents bedroom crying. "I can't sleep. My ear hurts too bad," I told my mother. She climbed out of bed and warmed some sweet oil and dropped it into my ear canal. The warmth felt good and I went back to sleep, only to awaken with the most horrible pain. A noise like a train went choo-choo-choo. Louder and louder it grew and the pressure accelerated until it was unbearable. I cried out, "Jesus help me!"

I felt a warm flow of blood and discharge spill from my ear on to my pillowcase. In the morning, my mother called the doctor for an appointment and he discovered that my eardrum had broken in the night. The only thing available to help was sulfa drugs. Antibiotics hadn't been discovered yet and sulfa drugs never really seemed to help. Most children outgrow ear problems but I never did. In my sixties I was upstairs wrapping Christmas gifts. All of a sudden I had the most unbearable pain. It was so intense I felt I might pass out. When I ran downstairs to tell my husband what happened, he said, "Go get in the car. I'm taking you to the hospital."

"But, honey, it isn't hurting now."

"You have blood running out your ear and down your neck," he replied." Go get in the car."

The doctors on duty told me that my eardrum had burst and gave me antibiotics. After the ear healed the doctor put tubes in my ears, and when they were present I had no more broken eardrums. When the tubes fell out they replaced them. I kept hoping maybe my ear problems were over. I praise God I can hear as well as I do with nothing but scar tissue for eardrums.

Ear problems were the first of many weakness that attacked my body, and I am still having the problem in my seventies. Right now it is nearly three in the morning on a cold rainy night in January and the pain in my ear is so excruciating I can't sleep. I don't have parents or even a mate to help me. I can't go to an urgent care or emergency hospital like I used to in San Jose. My pain grew worse until my eardrum broke again, the second time in my seventies.

God's grace and His strength are the power I need to enable me to accept whatever weakness strikes.

Until I have the joy of entering heaven where I will have ears with unbreakable eardrums, I will be consoled with the message God gave the Apostle Paul when he asked for help with a chronic malady. God told him,

My grace is sufficient for you, for my power is made perfect in weakness (2 Corinthians 12:9).

❀ Light Blindness

One Sunday after Sunday School, I was in the backyard playing with my brother and a few kids from the neighborhood. My brother, Henry, threw a sharp stick in the air. We all stood watching it go up and then it came down a lot faster than it had gone up. It landed right in my open eye and I passed out on the ground. Henry went for help. It was obvious to my parents I had splinters in my eye.

Somehow they got in touch with a doctor who could remove the splinters. They bundled me up and we dashed off to the doctor. He took one look at my eye and said, "I have to remove these splinters without any kind of an anesthetic. If she moves while I'm removing the splinter right on the line of her pupil, she'll be blind, so please do anything you know how, to get her to hold still."

"We'll buy you anything you want, Gwennie, if you'll hold perfectly still," Daddy told me.

"I want a new black dolly because I've played with Penny so much I've worn a hole in her head." All my white dolls were just like new because I never played with them, even though I was white too. The other thing I asked for was a chocolate bar.

I told my parents I wouldn't move and I could see the doctor working on my eye.

I can't remember being afraid, because I knew Jesus was with me. When the doctor finished removing all the splinters, he bandaged my eye and said to leave the bandages until the following Friday and then come back to see him.

Friday came and Mom took me back to see the doctor. He removed the bandages, covered my good eye and asked, "Can you see anything?"

I answered quite honestly, "No." The doctor told Mom the other eye would no doubt go blind out of sympathy for the hurt eye. He told her there were fine schools for the blind and talked about where they were located. It seemed settled that I was blind in the injured eye and would eventually go blind in the other eye. The doctor bandaged my eye again to keep it clean.

When we got home from the doctor's office, Mom told Daddy about what had happened and Daddy asked me, "Gwennie, couldn't you see anything?"

"No, Daddy, I couldn't see a thing with that bright light shining in my eye." Daddy started to laugh, and then Mom understood, too.

"You said you saw a bright light? That means you can see. You're not blind," Daddy told me.

"Yes, I did see something like a big flashlight shining right in my eye, but I couldn't see anything else," I told my father. "Do you mean I'm not blind like the doctor said? Can you take off the bandage so I can look around and see things?"

Daddy removed the bandage carefully so he could put it back on. The accident had not taken my vision away. "Daddy, I can see you and Mom and everything in the room!" God had helped me through being deaf and blind. He was the One I turned to when I needed someone to talk to and He was the One I thanked for taking care of me.

I loved to listen when my mother and my Sunday School teachers read from the Bible, and as I grew older I loved to read it myself and I believed what the Bible said.

Every year in Sunday School I received an award for handing in the most prepared homework and for answering the most questions correctly. One of the gifts I received was a picture of Jesus holding a baby lamb with sheep all around Him called, "The Good Shepherd." On the back is written, "I won this on September 18, 1938." It still hangs in my bathroom more than sixty years later.

I never had to be asked to do my Sunday School home work. I needed someone to help me read the Bible when I was very young, but after I learned to read I loved looking up things in the Bible. I'm sure my habit as a youngster helped make my relationship with God so important to me today.

Even when I am old and gray, do not forsake me, O God, till I declare your power to the next generation, your might to all who are to come (Psalm 71:18).

❀ Pleasing God Brings Love, Peace, and Joy

At eight years of age, with my mother's permission, I would go out to the garden and pick tomatoes, green beans, and corn. If we had a surplus I would take the tomatoes and polish them until they gleamed. Then I packaged them in little strawberry boxes and weighed them. I checked the prices in the stores and set my prices a little lower. I sold only the perfect produce and gave more than a pound weight.

I had some good solid customers in my neighborhood and even beyond. I'd take their names and phone numbers, and I would call them whenever I had the produce they wanted. I collected a tidy sum of money for an eight-year-old and I turned most of it over to my mother, hoping for her approval. I asked only to keep a small percentage.

At fourteen, I took over my brother's paper route, and at fifteen, I found work at a hospital on the maternity floor doing the dishes and setting up trays for the next meal. I couldn't bear the sound of the mothers' screams when the babies were delivered. I vowed not to scream when my babies were born.

I watched the newspaper for jobs. I wasn't quite sixteen when I got a job at Hollywood Hats. I seemed to have the knack of knowing just what hat would look wonderful on different shapes of faces. I'd sell as many as three hats to a customer and my boss was happy with me. I wasn't even working on a commission and I kept the cash register jingling. One reason customers always returned to me was that they knew I'd tell them the truth. If a hat didn't do anything for them I told them so. They felt they could trust me. I enjoyed waiting on customers and keeping them happy.

When I was in my late forties I found something else that filled my life with joy. I heard one of our ministers say: "Jesus' life is the only life acceptable to God." I wanted my life to be acceptable to God, so I prayed and asked my heavenly Father to allow Jesus to come live His life in and through me. I enjoyed many special moments filled with joy from that day on. Shortly thereafter, I heard an inner urging to *write, write, write.*

After losing three jobs in a row under strange circumstances, I went out and bought a typewriter and sat down and said, "All right, Lord, You show me what to write." My first article was accepted on its second submission. From then on, nearly every article I've written has appeared in at least one magazine, many in two, some in four and one article has been in seven magazines over the years.

It is not because of me. It is because Christ lives in me and His Holy Spirit is guiding what I write. My articles are used by many denominations, and have appeared in thirty-five different Christian magazines, Sunday School papers, and even in a few devotional booklets. I know there is power in the truth and God's Word is truth.

I started out trying to make my mother happy and then I worked to please people. What I had wanted all along was to please God and learn about His unconditional love for me. It's what everyone wants—to be loved by God, even though we don't deserve it. God waited patiently for me to come to Him, and give Him first place in my life, doing what He wanted me to do. Writing and speaking with those people God urges me to communicate with, brings me great joy. Slowly, I built an extremely close relationship with my Lord and Savior, Jesus Christ.

I found the peace described in the Bible. It is beyond human understanding. Also, I know a joy I've never known before. Writing fulfills me as a person and gives me a purpose for living. I want to be God's servant and delight myself in Him.

Meanwhile, He's given me the desires of my heart by allowing me to travel to places all over the world, places I never dreamed I'd ever see. God is faithful to those who love Him and He is to be trusted in all things.

We speak as men approved by God to be entrusted with the gospel. We are not trying to please men but God, who tests our hearts (1 Thessalonians 2:4).

❀ A Key to Wisdom

My dad, a ruggedly handsome man with a muscular physique, had a rare ability of storytelling. He told us about his riding the rails, lying on the underneath side of trains just like a hobo, hitching rides to different parts of the country, but most generally to Colorado.

"One meets some pretty low-down, crusty pole cats traveling the rails. Sometimes I took a real beating," he told us. He was tough and strong and loved adventure. Even though he got into some pretty bad fights, he always seemed to come out on top. His parents had both died before he was fifteen, and he was riding the rails to see the country and find out who he really was and where he'd like to settle down.

When I was little I loved to hear my Dad's stories. I also loved for my

Dad to hoist me up on his shoulders and carry me to the park where he pushed me higher and higher on the swings. I didn't like it when the swing got so high that it stopped for a moment, and then seemed to jerk and fall straight down feeling like it would drop to the ground. The more I'd yell for Daddy to stop, the higher he'd push me. One day I went up higher and higher and up over the top. I would never recommend this since I might have fallen out and really been hurt. However, after I'd once faced what I dreaded would happen and lived through it, I wasn't afraid anymore. Facing our fears with Jesus' strength, helps us enjoy the abundant life.

My husband and I were floating down a river in Texas with Joy, our daughter in Christ. She planned this wonderful outing and it was a beautiful day, and the water was warm. We each sat in a huge inner tube and I kept hearing a falls up ahead and it frightened me. *What if I should go over the falls?* When we arrived at the falls it was easy to avoid, but I decided to face my fear. I saw a few young men going over the falls in their inner tubes. I talked to one of them who told me how it was done.

I did the very thing I'd felt so afraid of doing. It was pretty scary when all that water came up and hit me in the face, but it felt wonderful to know Jesus had given me the strength to face my fear and overcome it by going over a fifteen foot waterfall in a tube, at an advanced age. Fear can be destructive, but when we fear God by giving Him reverence and respect because of who He is, we can have a much better relationship with Him.

Sometimes God allows us to go through scary and difficult times in our lives so that we may learn to call on Him for help and surrender our difficulties into His care.

There is only One we need to fear or stand in awe of, and that is God. How is it possible not to reverence the Majesty of the One who created this glorious world, knowing He is all powerful, all knowing, and all wise? Once we learn to give God the proper place in our lives, we grow to love and trust Him in all things.

He is a loving Father. However some take this to mean that because He loves me I may do as I please. This is where the fear or reverence for God's authority needs to be remembered.

If Lot's wife had feared God's power she would not have become a pillar of salt.

The fear of the Lord is the beginning of wisdom (Psalm 111:10a).

He [the Lord] *will be the sure foundation for your times, a rich store of salvation and wisdom and knowledge; the fear of the Lord is the key to this treasure* (Isaiah 33:6).

Maturing in the Word

"Mom, I'm scheduled to start confirmation class at our church, right after we go back to school," Henry announced at dinner one night.

I loved learning about the Bible. "I sure wish I could go to confirmation along with Henry," I told my mother.

"You know, Gwennie, that might be a good idea since you have so far to go and you'll be coming home late—around six o'clock alone. If you took the class now, you could come home with Henry," Mom answered.

"I don't want my little sister tagging along with me," Henry told her. "Besides, she's not old enough to keep up with my class."

It took us three buses to get to St. Paul's Lutheran Church since we didn't have a car. Sometimes we walked to church. My mother knew I'd be starting confirmation in two years and didn't want me coming home alone in the dark during the winter months, and she asked if I could take the class with my brother.

The Board of Elders had to make that decision. After conferring, they decided that since I prepared my Sunday School lessons so faithfully, I would probably be able to keep up with children two years older than myself. Confirmation classes were held threes time a week for two years, and I loved learning all of the important Bible passages Martin Luther had placed in the Small Catechism.

What a wonderful privilege it was to have Pastor Jesse for our teacher. He not only believed what he taught us, he also wanted to be a good example.

One of the mothers told her son she wanted him to stop smoking and her son asked her, "If Pastor Jesse smokes, why can't I?" The woman called Pastor Jesse and repeated what her son had said. Pastor Jesse quit smoking immediately.

The way Pastor Jesse helped us learn our Bible passages and the reference where it was found in the Bible was, if one student missed even one word of the passage or any part of the text where it was found, if the next student could recite the passage perfectly, they moved up one seat while the other student who said one word wrong would move down. There were eight kids in the class and my brother and I generally sat in the first, second, or third seat.

When Pastor Jesse explained things we could understand them. He taught us about tithing. I was only ten when he told us to take the amount we received for allowance and give ten percent to the church. I received a dollar allowance. This meant giving ten cents.

I would divide the ten cents and put eight cents in the side of our envelope toward supporting the church and two cents in the side for missions. This habit is something I'll always be grateful I started. I am certain that the wonderful blessings God gave me later in life came as a result of my being faithful in giving at least ten percent back to God.

It was extremely touching to see someone as large as Pastor Jesse cry when it was our last class before confirmation. He cried when he told us how hard it was for him to bid us farewell as students. I knew he cared about each of us and we felt very close to him. He was a great teacher and a marvelous preacher as well. He would see us at Walther League meetings and at church, and I think he became as attached to us as we did to him.

Never again, to my knowledge, did the St. Paul Lutheran Church of St. Joseph, Missouri put another group through the intense studies and testing we were given. However, I'm happy I was part of that class because it gave me a wonderful grasp of what Christianity really is. We were put through three hours of constant questions from the Board of Elders, before we were actually confirmed in church. My brother and I did well. We had to really know the entire Catechism which was mostly Bible passages. It also taught the Ten Commandments, and what they meant, the meaning of the Apostles' Creed, and the Lord's Prayer, the meaning of grace, and what a sacrament was. It told us how to live a Christian life. The adults also had to go through confirmation to join the church. However, they didn't have to learn all the memory work.

After being passed by the board we had to answer questions during the Confirmation Service on Palm Sunday. Questions covered any point we'd touched during our two years of intensive study. When the pastor asked us a question we had to stand in our white robes, face the congregation, and give the answers.

One young man, who had been very sharp in class missed at least half of the questions he was asked. I don't believe my brother Henry or I missed any. This was a very important part of my life. For Lutherans, confirmation is when the children who were baptized as infants are able to say, "yes" to the questions their parents and godparents answered for them at their baptism. Now the teenager has the responsibility of learning about God, and answering for themselves that they intend to hold the Word of God as holy, and to be faithful to its teaching.

This was one of the most important days in my life and one I'll never forget nor ignore. I think it is exactly what young people are missing today.

Live as children of light… and find out what pleases the Lord (Ephesians 5:8b,10).

❀ An Extraordinary Gift from God

In 1939 when I was almost ten and my brother Henry was twelve, our parents told us they had a wonderful surprise. Mother and Dad never looked happier. "We're going to have another baby," Mom told us.

"Yes, Henry and Gwennie, you are going to have a baby brother or sister. Isn't that good news?" Dad asked.

I couldn't wait to hold a new little baby. When people told me that having a new baby in the house was going to put my nose out of joint, I looked in the mirror and wondered what they meant. I thought, *My nose isn't out of joint. It looks the way it always has.* Why should I mind that I would no longer be the youngest in the family? I was going to hold and love a new baby. *What could be better than that?*

I'll never forget the night Gloria was born, because my mother gave birth at home. It was a breech birth which meant the baby came out doubled in two. Mother screamed so loud I was sure everyone in a two block radius knew she was giving birth. I promised myself *I will not scream during childbirth.*

My new little sister, Gloria, had platinum blonde hair and dark brown eyes. To me she was the most beautiful little girl I'd ever seen. I loved to hold her, feed her, and even change her. I couldn't have loved her more. She was extraordinary and very bright. Mother started showing her pictures of the presidents and telling her who they were. When Mom asked her to point at President Lincoln or George Washington, she could point them out. Every day Mother would tell her another president's name and then ask her to point him out. She never missed and some of those presidents looked so much alike in their pictures, I was amazed that she never missed pointing out the correct president.

It concerned all of us when she started crying whenever she bent to sit down. Mom took her to the doctor and he told her she just worried too much, Gloria was fine. By the time she was twenty months old, she seemed to be in pain much of the time. Mother and Dad took her to another doctor who took a group of lab tests and found out what was wrong with our darling baby.

I'd never heard of leukemia before, but the tests said she had acute leukemia. It seemed her red and white blood corpuscles were disappearing and she needed blood transfusions. Dad had the correct type of blood and he wanted Gloria to have his blood. When they had already taken more blood from him than legally allowed, he started eating ground up raw liver hoping to replenish his blood supply so he could give her all the transfusions she needed.

Gloria had to be taken to the hospital when she was twenty-two months old. She never came back home. Her death was more difficult than anything I'd ever gone through. I don't think my mom or dad had any idea how I suffered from losing my sister, because they were in such pain themselves. Our little darling had gone home to be with Jesus so young.

Our large church was packed for the funeral. Children were pall bearers and the children's choir sang several hymns. Mother chose "What a Friend We Have in Jesus," to be sung and many times afterward when we sang that song, I broke down and cried so excessively that I had to leave church. After my marriage when I was living in San Francisco, I was sitting with my Sunday School class and when we sang "What a Friend We Have in Jesus," I started crying so hard I had to leave. I wish I'd paid more attention to the words in the second line of that hymn, "All our sins and griefs to bear!" Jesus had already borne my grief. I needed to release my sorrow and give it to Him.

One good thing came out of Gloria's death. Through Pastor Jesse's visits with my mom and dad during this stressful period, my daddy built a real friendship with the pastor and he started attending church. He listened to Pastor Jesse more than he ever had to any pastor before.

Going to church as a family was something my mother, my brother, and I had all prayed for, for years. Through my sister's death our family received new life.

And we know that in all things God works for the good of those who love him, who have been called according to his purpose (Romans 8:28).

❀ Moments of Terror

Walking home alone from Lindbergh Grade School, I took the same short-cut across a large empty lot that I did every evening. All this lot contained was a huge billboard like the ones we now see lifted high in the air along highways. A sort of scaffolding was built under it to raise it off the ground, putting it just above eye level and high enough kids couldn't deface it on their way home from school.

I had no idea that fifteen or twenty kids were lying in wait ready to ambush me.

I was a little surprised when I saw three boys, too old to attend grade school, slither out from behind the billboard and head straight for me. Then I noticed a bunch of grade school kids running out from behind the billboard, and before I knew what was happening they made a tight circle around me. Terror struck when I saw a switchblade knife opened and pointed in my direction. My terror intensified when I glimpsed another knife and still another switchblade knife opened with the blades pointed straight at me. Now I was filled with terror.

Were they planning to use those knives on me?

"What do you want?" I asked shaking. My heart was pounding wildly. One of the bigger bullies stepped toward me. He reminded me of a pit bull about ready to attack. *If only I had a muzzle to put over his menacing face,* I thought. When he opened his mouth to speak I expected to hear a growl. I was afraid to hear what he was about to say.

"I've got questions for you to answer," he snarled.

"About what?" I asked full of dread. I had no idea what to expect.

"You go to a church with a cross on it don't you?" he asked accusingly. *What kind of question was that?* "Yeah, I attend a church with a cross."

"You're a Catholic, aren't you?"

"No, I'm not a Catholic, I go to a Lutheran church, but I still don't see what difference that should make to you." I was breathing much easier now.

"But you admit that your church has a cross on top of it, right?"

"Right. I attend a church with a steeple that has a cross on top of it. Why shouldn't a church have a cross on it? Jesus died on a cross for the bad things you and I do. At church we call those things sin."

When I spoke about Jesus it didn't seem to faze these kids. It was Catholics they were prejudiced against, not Jesus. At first I thought I was going to be hauled behind that billboard and murdered, but when I heard those kids firing a barrage of questions centering around a church with a cross I became filled with indignation. All I could think about was, *I've got to get these kids' thinking straightened out so they won't pull this on someone else.* I had started confirmation class and I knew about Luther as a monk, standing against those who wanted to kill him. Luther stood up for what he believed and I knew I had to stand up for what I believed.

"All I've been hearing from you is that you are prejudiced against me because I attend a church with a cross on its steeple."

I looked around and all the kids were quieted down and were listening.

"Now, I'm going to tell you what I believe and when I get through you can decide what you want to do." This was my first attempt at teaching and I felt it was very important for me to say things forcefully to make an impact on these kids.

"God wants all people to be saved, including you. He sent Jesus, His only Son, to earth to die for your sins and for mine, because none of us are perfect, but Jesus was without sin. He hadn't done anything wrong but He died because people told lies about Him. Now, if we believe that Jesus was God's Son, and that He died on that cross, and we believe He rose again from the dead on Easter Sunday, we don't have to be afraid of dying because our soul lives on in heaven where there is no sickness or sin. Now don't you see why we love Jesus? The cross just reminds us how He died for us. And there were many witnesses to the fact He died and even more that He arose from the dead. These are historical facts.

"Churches don't have to have a cross on them but no one should gang up on me because I attend a church with a cross. And Catholics believe in Jesus, too. Maybe you need to decide for yourselves what you believe before you gang up on anybody else."

I was no longer afraid of them and they knew it. They were just a bunch of prejudiced kids, ignorant about the truth.

They knew I meant what I said, and with my faith they couldn't intimidate me because I knew God and I knew Jesus was my Savior; and even if they killed me I'd still go on living only in a better place. I had realized I must be so emphatic in what I said that these bullies would never again brow-beat someone about the church they attended. When I got through, they certainly knew more about what Christianity was than they had when this all started, because I had made my beliefs quite clear.

When I finished it was quiet. I watched those holding knives fold the blade inside very quietly, and then they dropped the knives in their pockets. They weren't going to interrogate me any more. The rest of the boys, their heads hanging in shame, scrambled after the older boys.

A few of the girls walked over to talk with me and I had the distinct feeling that the girls were proud of the way I quieted those bullies. Those girls must have been the ones to tell the older boys where I attended church. I don't know how they would have known since my church was located a long way from the grade school.

To this day I don't know how this all came to happen but I knew that day, that prejudice must be stopped if we wanted to keep our country free.

For what I received I passed on to you as of first importance: that Christ died for our sins according to the Scriptures, that he was buried, that he was raised on the third day according to the Scriptures, and that he appeared to Peter, and then to the twelve. After that he appeared to more than five hundred of the brothers at the same time, most of whom are still living, though some have fallen asleep [died]. *Then he appeared to James, then to all the apostles and last of all he appeared to me, also* [Paul], *as to one abnormally born* (1 Corinthians 15:3-8).

2

Memories of the Teenage Years

Now this is eternal life: that they may know you, the only true God, and Jesus Christ, whom you have sent (John 17:3).

The Pain of Losing Grandma

My Brother's Kindred Spirit

The Loss of a Friend

Following in His Footprints

My Faith Gave Me Courage

Resisting Temptation

"I have made you known to them, and will continue to make you known in order that the love you have for me may be in them and that I myself may be in them"
(John 17:26; Jesus praying to His heavenly Father for believers).

🌼 The Pain of Losing Grandma

I always loved to visit my grandparents' home. It sat nestled on a hill with lovely trees surrounding it. There must have been forty cement steps to enter their yard the front way. I loved to go there, because my grandmother was a sensational cook and her pot roasts were just the way I liked them, and her wilted lettuce salads and her red cabbage and other German dishes were delicious.

However, the things she baked were the best of all. The caramel covered cinnamon rolls, German cookies, stollen, a Christmas bread, and coffee cakes were my favorites. The house always smelled of fresh baked bread and cookies. The way my grandmother thanked me for washing her windows or doing other chores for her was to slip me some of those baked goodies. It was fun doing jobs for her. She appreciated me so much.

My grandmother was what model Christians should be. I never heard her say an unkind word to or about anyone, even when Grandpa was quite irritable.

I was there when she had her second heart attack. The doctor pronounced her dead. My grandfather started crying and rubbing my grandmother's arms and legs.

"Anna, Anna, don't leave me. I need you," he pleaded. I stared in amazement when her eyes fluttered open. Her face had a glorious radiance for someone who had just been pronounced dead.

"Louis," she said, "I've just seen heaven and it is beautiful! Please don't bring me back if I should go again. Promise me you won't!"

Grandpa promised and a few hours later she died again and he didn't call her back. My grandmother, the person I loved most after Gloria, left to return to heaven. I knew I'd never be afraid to die. My grandmother never lied and she said heaven was beautiful, so I know she joined my sister, Gloria, there.

I needed someone I could talk with, about losing my sister and my grandmother, the two people I loved so dearly. My parents were not aware of my grief and I refused to trouble them. On the outside I acted like everything was fine but on the inside the pain of my grief was almost unbearable. I didn't think Christians were supposed to be sad because their loved ones were in a better place. If I could have just broken down and let everyone know how much I missed my sister and my grandmother. I often thought about dying myself so I wouldn't hurt so bad. I remembered my grandmother saying how beautiful heaven was and I wanted to go with my loved ones, but I knew suicide was a sin against God's commandment not to kill. However, I thought about ways I could put an end to my misery.

I really don't think adults realize how sad younger children or teenagers feel when loved ones die. It was impossible for me to express the loneliness I felt for them. If only I had understood that I could talk it over with Jesus and that He would give me His strength to bear the deaths of my loved ones. Our Pastor Jesse probably would have been happy to help me, too, but it's hard to deal with. Youth counselors need to know that children who have lost a loved one are hurting real bad and get them to talk about how they feel. Friends of the child or a teenager who's lost someone in the family, might help a great deal by drawing the young person out and maybe sharing their own experience if they've lost a family member.

My soul is weary with sorrow; strengthen me according to your Word (Psalm 119:28).

🌺 My Brother's Kindred Spirit

Two years after Gloria died, when I was fourteen, Henry and I learned Mom was expecting another baby—someone to replace Gloria.

What we got was a boy—Ronald Jesse!

"Here we wanted a precious baby girl like Gloria and just look what we got." My mom held Ronnie up for everyone to see. "Doesn't he look like a rough and tough little prize fighter, with his hair standing on end?"

He not only looked rough and tough he acted out that role. I remember him running into my ankles with his "tailor-tot" he rode around the house. It wasn't entirely accidental because he'd laugh and laugh when I hobbled around with wounded ankles.

At that time my folks still lived in St.Joseph, Missouri. However, they later moved to Grand Junction, Colorado, saying they'd meet us half way. My Uncle Alfred lived there.

I saw Ronnie as he grew. He became an uncle at five years of age, when my daughter, Terry was born. She adored her Uncle Ronnie and they had loads of fun playing together. After Cindy was born she too, loved her Uncle Ronnie with a special type of love. I remember him polishing Cindy's white shoes and sitting them outside of her door on a Saturday night ready for Sunday School the next day. He placed them there after she went to sleep so she wouldn't know he was the elf who polished her shoes. He did his act of kindness without ever telling Cindy. Later Cindy learned from her grandmother it was Ronnie who polished her shoes. He had love in him but tried to keep up a tough front to go along with Mother's description of him. He always tried to sound tough and he talked awful, but really underneath he was quite intelligent and very kind.

By talking awful, I don't mean cursing or using profanity. I never heard Ronnie use profanity or nasty words. However, he enjoyed saying outrageous things to people who came to my mom's floral shop. After looking at an ample woman who came into the flower shop Ronnie said, "Boy, you're fat!" He often hid his sweet spirit by making shocking and tactless statements and producing loud burps. I honestly think he felt it was expected of "tough little Ronnie."

Even though he refused to turn in homework, in school he made fairly good grades because he nearly always made A's and B's on his final tests, showing he had heard what his teachers had been saying. He also heard Mother telling him repeatedly that he wasn't exactly what she was looking for when he was born.

Later he would tell me, "When you're told every day of your life that you aren't what your mother wanted, it really does something to you." How well I knew!

When Ronnie was fourteen he drove a neighbor's truck down over the cliffs and he couldn't get it back up. He finally told Daddy. Daddy looked down at the bottom of the cliff and said, "Well, son, you got it there, now you have to get it out." And Ronnie got it out. My dad thought he must have taken the truck apart and reassembled it piece by piece, but he would never tell us how he got it out.

When Ronnie got out of school and home from the army, he built rental duplexes on some of my folks' property. He built the refrigeration units for the flowers in Mother's flower shop and he delivered flowers for Mother. One day Mother told me, "You know I'd wanted a little girl to take Gloria's place when Ronnie was born, but she could never have done for us all the things Ronnie has. God knew best when He blessed us with Ronnie." I doubt that Mother ever told Ronnie this.

When teenagers get into so much trouble, I remember how Ronnie didn't get into drugs, smoking pot, cigarettes or anything else habit forming. He never drank anything stronger than root beer. I never saw him take an alcoholic drink.

One of the ways Ronnie showed hospitality to visitors was to take people for a drive closer and closer to the edge of some thirty to fifty foot cliffs about half a mile from their home. He loved to give people a real scare. First he would drive right to the edge of the cliff. Everyone would gasp with relief when he stopped just in time. At that moment Ronnie would let the car roll over the edge. That's when the screaming started and when Ronnie got his kicks. Once he took me on his motorcycle over the edge of the cliffs and I chose to jump off and roll part way down the cliff.

Ronnie had practiced that trip over the cliffs many times and I think he'd worn ridges in the side of the cliff so he could drive down with no danger. Many times his kids were in the car with the visitors. To this day no one has ever been hurt going over the cliffs with Ronnie.

One of the funniest things he told us about happened while he was in the army. One night while he was on guard duty, he waited until lights out and everyone was asleep. Then he took fireworks he'd bought from a town nearby, and fastened them together and strung them throughout the barracks. At the appropriate time he lit the fuse and in the middle of the night fire crackers started to explode. The men leaped from their bunks and watched flabbergasted at a display of fireworks right in their sleeping quarters. And who do you suppose they called to investigate the matter? Why Ronnie, of course.

My brother is probably a genius because the service wanted him in the Intelligence Corps. He would have driven them mad. Besides he didn't care for the service. He liked his life at home doing what he wanted when he wanted to do it.

When Ronnie finally got married, he turned out to be a caring father to four sons. However, they sometimes say, "Oh, Dad!" when he makes one of his outrageous comments.

I've never forgotten the great bunny hutch he built for his kids' rabbits. It was an elaborate runway, probably an eighth of a block long that gave the bunnies lots of places to run and kept them from feeling penned up.

Ronnie never missed a Sunday going to Sunday School or church in all the years we visited back there. And he and his wife took their four sons to church despite their not providing a nursery with babysitters for young children.

When my daughter, Cindy, goes to visit Ronnie she and her children have a really good time. The kids love being around Uncle Ron. He calls kids hippies if they have long hair, and he always has wise cracks for everyone, but underneath it all lingers his sweet, good-natured spirit. God made each of us unique. We are one of a kind and God doesn't make mistakes.

God loves and accepts each of us as we are. I'm sure Mom did love Ronnie even if it did sound like he wasn't what she'd wanted. I love him, and I'm proud of all the imagination, inventiveness and the ingenuity he's shown throughout his life.

And he is fun to be around, too!

"Because he loves me," says the Lord, "I will rescue him; I will protect him, for he acknowledges my name. He will call upon me, and I will answer him;… I will deliver him and honor him. With long life will I satisfy him and show him my salvation" (Psalm 91:14-16).

❀ The Loss of a Friend

Carl, the president of our church youth group had gone swimming and dived head first into water too shallow and broke his neck. He died almost instantly.

I remember Carl well, because the Board of Elders had chosen him to be Joseph the same year they chose me to portray Mary. It was an honor for me to portray the mother of our Lord, and Carl was a fine choice to be Joseph. I was pleased to kneel beside him with baby Jesus in the manger.

And now he too, was dead. Losing such a good friend hit me like a bolt of lightning. One evening Carl presided over our youth group and the next evening he was dead from a broken neck. I cried because these three people left a void in my life. I knew we would be reunited in heaven. My belief in God that Jesus had paid for our sins on the cross, and my being certain of an afterlife helped to comfort me.

Still, I needed someone I could talk to, a person who would listen and not judge or condemn me for the way I felt. I needed someone to share my grief with me. Even my brother, Henry, two years older than I, did not speak to me about the grief he must have felt. We could have been such a comfort for each other. I know that he had to have been badly shaken. Why can't families talk to each other about how they feel when parents, siblings, or friends die? We need to share our deep feelings with each other. However,

I'm sure that our belief in God grew stronger through these deaths. My brother and I had a strong faith in God because we did talk everything over with Him in prayer.

What a weight was lifted from my shoulders the day I asked Jesus to carry the burden of my sin and griefs. I don't know if Henry learned to give Jesus His griefs and I can't ask him now, because he, too, has gone to be with the Lord.

"I tell you the truth, whoever hears my Word and believes him who sent me has eternal life and will not be condemned; he has crossed over from death to life" (John 5:24).

✿ Following in His Footprints

"Heavenly Father, please help me get to the top of this steep road," I prayed. It was beginning to get dark and I knew my parents would be worried about me.

My sixteen-year-old brother, Henry, had needed someone to carry his paper route. It was the longest route in St. Joseph, Missouri. I had volunteered to take over for him while he was recuperating from a bad case of the mumps. I hadn't expected to be carrying papers when the ground was slick as glass.

First it had snowed, and then it had rained and frozen over. In order to reach a few isolated houses I had to go down a steep country road. Going down had been easy. By sitting down it had become a block-long slide.

Getting back up the steep incline was another matter. I tried time after time, but even crawling on my hands and knees I'd slip backward. I'd tried grabbing hold of the tops of small shrubs buried in the snow at the side of the road, but they crumbled in my mittens. I could get out another way by hiking over the railroad tracks, but I wouldn't be able to make it home by dark.

"Gwennie, is that you?" my father shouted to me from the top of the hill.

"It's me, Daddy," I yelled back, happy that he'd come.

As the familiar figure of my father drew closer, I felt a deep sense of relief. I knew he would be able to help me. "I was beginning to think I'd never get home tonight. I just couldn't seem to get to the top of this road no matter what I did," I told my father.

"When it became so late your mother and I figured you were stuck somewhere. Grab hold of me, Gwennie. I'll get you to the top." I felt secure with my father's arms around me, pulling me toward the top. My daddy's size thirteen shoes were able to dig into the snow, so I could follow in his footprints. About a third of the way up the steep incline we were doing so well I stepped out ahead of my father. As I did, I slipped and my father and I went shooting backwards down the road, laughing all the way.

Once again we started up the steep road. This time we went even farther. Once more I grew confident enough to pull out ahead of my father. My feet slipped out from under me again and I fell, pulling my father down with me. He landed with a thud. When we could stop laughing, my father sat grinning at me. "She's a slick one tonight, Gwennie. If you want to get home tonight, I think you'd better let me do the leading."

Many years later reading my Bible, I thought about that night. I could see the same truth applies to our Lord Jesus. When He's leading, I don't slip. It's when I pull out ahead of Him, relying on my own strength, I'm sure to slip and fall.

And he [Jesus] *is able to keep you from slipping and falling away, and to bring you, sinless and perfect, into his glorious presence with mighty shouts of everlasting joy* (Jude 1:24-25 TLB).

*This article was published in the January 12, 1992, *The Lookout*, Standard Publishing and in the April 18, 1993, *Live*, Gospel Publishing House /Assemblies of God.

❀ My Faith Gave Me Courage

"Henry, I really enjoyed carrying your paper route," I told my brother after filling in for him while he had the mumps. "Why don't you just go get a better job for yourself and let me keep the paper route?" I asked him. That's just what he did and I became the official carrier for the longest route in St. Joseph, Missouri.

Imagine my surprise to find an article about me on the front page of the Sunday paper. The headline read: "Girl Owes Job to Brother's Mumps." It told all about my being the first girl paper carrier in St. Joseph, Missouri, and how I'd filled in for my brother and then taken over the route.

This was a route that had to be carried by foot. No bike could go through cow pastures and over and under fences. One morning I stepped on something that moved. I looked down and under my foot was a long black snake. Unlike most girls, I was not afraid of snakes so the incident did not cause me alarm.

Wanted by God

I did feel fearful each morning when I walked down a long road in the dark that stretched out over two blocks with nothing but trees on either side. There were no houses or sidewalks, just tree limbs that looked like long arms reaching out to grab me. It was especially frightening before I got a helper and I had to walk that road alone. I started praying before I started down the road and I prayed all the way for God's protection. It would have been so easy for a man to hide and jump out and grab me and there was no place I could run for help.

I still remembered how a man had followed me one day when I walked to town. I was on the boulevard system with no houses to run to. First he called from across the street to ask if I wanted a ride and then he did a U turn and started down the street on the side where I was walking. He tried to get me to come to his car, and then he got out of his car and started chasing me; but I outran him, and I ran until I got into one of the main stores in town and then I collapsed into a nearby chair.

Faith in my almighty heavenly Father was my only comfort as I faced that long walk on my route each morning. I prayed for God's angels to guard and protect me from harm and keep me safe. Knowing that I could talk with God all the way, made that scary walk and each day of my difficult teenage years much easier.

By getting up at 3:00 in the morning, I could be back home by 6:30. After I enlisted the help of my friend, Lillian, we could carry the papers and be back home at 6:00 to fall into bed for a little more sleep. We carried not only the morning paper but the evening and the Sunday papers, too. I knew God's angels were nearby to protect me from harm.

On another day I was riding my bike down to the store to get meat for dinner. On that particular day I was getting ready to cross a very wide and busy street on my way home. I looked to the right and then to the left and I saw a car coming, but it was a long way off. I figured I had plenty of time to get across the street. I hopped on my bike and started across. Somewhere in the middle of the street the car and I collided. To this day I don't know exactly where my bike was hit. I only know I ended up on the sidewalk on the other side of the street. I'd gone one way, my bike another, and the meat flew out of the basket another way. My bike seat landed just beyond my bike. Our sidewalks had extremely high curbs and it has always amazed me that everything ended up on the sidewalk over that high curb. I'd collided with the car on the side facing the other side of the street. I had to literally fly through the air to end that far away and up over the curb on the sidewalk.

The man who hit me came back to look at me and he asked, "Are you dead?"

I've always wondered what he would have done if I'd answered, "Yes."

I was shaking so hard I could barely walk. Somehow, someone helped get the seat back on my bike, the basket attached more securely and the meat in the basket again. I couldn't ride my bike. I had to push it home because I was shaking too hard. I never told Mom what had happened to me, because I figured she'd probably take my bike away.

I do know one thing for sure, and that is that heavenly angels guarded me during my bike accident and also walking down those two lonely blocks on my paper route.

For he will command his angels concerning you to guard you in all your ways; they will lift you up in their hands, so that you will not strike your foot against a stone (Psalm 91:11-12).

❀ Resisting Temptation

I was invited to a party at Shirley's house. Since she was one of my closest friends, I decided to go. When I arrived, something didn't feel right. After awhile I realized Shirley's mother and father weren't home. Shirley and her older brother, Rick, were hosting the party alone.

After talking with my friends that were there, I noticed a bottle of booze being passed around. When it came to me I just passed it on.

Then the games started and one was a kissing game. I noticed some of the young people were getting a little too involved in the game. Then one of the guys I barely knew came toward me with his arms outstretched. I gathered he thought he was going to kiss me. I certainly didn't know him well enough to kiss him. When he came over and started to pull me to him, I took both of my hands, placed them against his chest and gave one big shove. He bounced off the opposite wall.

"Hey guys, you'd better leave Gwendolyn alone!" he warned.

About five minutes later I walked out. "This is no place for me to be," I told Shirley.

I learned at school the next day that after I had the courage to leave, a number of other kids left, too. My friend was mad at me for a long time after that night but it didn't bother me. I knew God was the one I wanted to please, not Shirley. Her party without any parents or chaperones present did not fit my idea of a good place to stay.

Submit yourselves, then, to God. Resist the devil, and he will flee from you (James 4:7).

3

Becoming a Teenage Bride

Children obey your parents in everything, for this pleases the Lord (Colossians 3:20).

 An Unexpected Letter

 My Parents Say, "Yes!"

 Our Honeymoon to San Francisco

But my righteous one will live by faith. And if he shrinks back, I will not be pleased with him [/her].
(Hebrews 10:38).

❦ An Unexpected Letter

Toward the end of the paper route a Model T used to sit in front of one of my customer's homes. Several mornings, my helper, Lillian and I even sat down in the seat to rest. It was fun sitting in that quaint old car. Then it was replaced with a Model A that had a rumble seat in back. We tried out the rumble seat, too. The people who lived in that house had their nephew, Harold, living with them for awhile and he owned the old cars.

His aunt's house was up at least thirty stairs so they couldn't see us even if they'd been up, but it was probably 5:30 in the morning when we got that far on our route. We'd see Harold driving home from work some evenings while we delivered the evening paper and he always waved to us. Suddenly the cars disappeared and we no longer saw Harold driving his old car anymore. His cousins told us he'd joined the Navy.

One day there was a letter in our mail box stamped U.S. Navy and it was addressed to me. I tore the envelope open and read: "Standing on the lowest form of conventional integrity, I am endeavoring to become better acquainted with you." It appeared that Harold had quite a command of the English vocabulary and he'd written a very pleasant letter asking that I write to him.

Harold, the young man who sent me the letter from the Navy was the one who'd owned those old cars we'd sat in early in the morning.

Naturally I answered his letter because I was already writing to several boys from our church, and after all that was something I could do for the war effort. I could write so a few of our service men would receive letters. When I wrote, I told Harold I was fifteen since my birthday was only a week away. After I wrote and told him I had a birthday, he asked how it felt to be sweet sixteen. I avoided answering that question because I figured he wouldn't write me again if he knew I was only fifteen.

I wondered what he'd thought when he'd stopped to ask me if I wanted a ride with him one night, and I answered with, "I should say not!" I didn't even know his name at the time, and it wasn't my habit of climbing into cars with strangers. He later told me he respected me for answering as I did.

Originally, Harold thought I was carrying papers to work my way through college. Because I stood five feet, nine inches tall, I was often taken for older, but I still attended high school. When I took care of small children, people often thought they were mine. At that age I felt looking older was a compliment. I felt flattered that a Navy man would write me.

While I was feeding my baby brother one day, my brother Henry teased me with, "Your sailor boyfriend is here."

Used to his teasing, I said, "Oh, sure he is!" I turned around and there stood Harold, whom I'd been corresponding with for about six months.

At that moment my baby brother, Ronnie, dumped his bowl of cereal and he picked up a handful and threw it at me. I dashed over, picked up a soggy dish cloth, wiped up the mess on Ronnie's tray and threw the cloth across the room into the kitchen sink. I felt a little strange when I saw some of the cereal flying off in Harold's direction.

When I lifted Ronnie out of his high chair and held him in my lap, he wet me. Without bothering to say where I was going or why, I ran from the room to change my clothes. I left Harold sitting on a chair in the middle of the kitchen. I'm surprised he didn't get up and leave. I was amazed that he even wrote me another letter after that visit.

After I got to know him much better, it seemed every time he wanted to kiss me when Ronnie was nearby, Ronnie would yell, "Mama, Mama, Mama."

We exchanged letters for several years and Harold had been home on two leaves, where we saw each other maybe three times. He gave me a watch when I became sixteen and my mother told him I couldn't accept such an expensive gift. Somehow Harold managed to convince my mother that my letters were worth more than that to him and he truly wanted me to have the watch, so I ended up wearing it.

Since Harold had been valedictorian when he graduated, I worked hard to make excellent grades. In Missouri, "E" was for Excellent, "S" for Superior, "M" for Medium, "I" for Inferior and "F" for Failure. In my eleventh and twelfth grades I managed to get an "E" average in all my classes. Since he was smart I wanted good grades.

When the war ended and Harold had been discharged, he wrote he was coming back to Missouri to visit me. He fell asleep in the car on the way back, and if there had not been sturdy, metal barriers on those high mountain roads he would have been killed or badly hurt.

He never had long to stay, because in the beginning he had to get back to the service, or he left to go visit his parents who lived in California at the time. Usually he came back for two to three days and it didn't give us much time to get acquainted. After the war, he had a job and he could only get off on short vacations. He was very quiet and hard to get acquainted with. My dad took him along to work with him one day to get to know him better. He came home and said: "How do you get that boy to talk to you? All he did with me was to answer my questions with yes or no, but I couldn't get him to say anything. I feel worn out from trying to get him to talk."

Harold wrote such long informative letters it seemed strange that he talked so little. He didn't believe in talking unless he had something worthwhile to say. His not wanting to talk or partake in outgoing activities was hard for me to accept. He'd talk when he had a point he wanted to get across. We sometimes think people will talk more when we know them better but quiet people don't change that much. I love to have someone to talk to and silent type people can become lonely companions.

A man who lacks judgment derides his neighbor, but a man of understanding holds his tongue (Proverbs 11:12).

❀ My Parents Say, "Yes!"

The war ended and Harold decided he wanted to live in California. He went there and got a job. We wrote to each other three or four times a week. Finally he wrote that he was coming back to see me.

After taking me to the movies one evening we were sitting in the car. Harold was unusually quiet. He never had much to say, but tonight he said even less than usual.

"A penny for your thoughts," I broke the silence.

"Will you marry me?" he asked.

I wasn't expecting a proposal. Naturally it made me feel important that a twenty-two-year-old wanted to marry me. I was only seventeen. I didn't feel I even knew Harold. It was so sudden that I told him I had to think about it. I guess I had a funny look on my face when he took me home that evening because Mom asked:

"What's wrong?"

"Harold asked me to marry him tonight," I told her.

"What did you say?" Mom asked.

"I didn't give him an answer yet," I replied. However, I had more reservations about marrying Harold than my mother had. She said she'd go down with us when we got our marriage license and give her permission since I was not yet eighteen.

One night after dating Harold, I felt sure I didn't want to marry him because he smoked and his breath and the smell of smoke on his clothes was so strong, it made me feel sick. I had never been around anyone who smoked, because my dad and brother didn't and neither had my mother ever smoked, so that I had no idea how being around the smell constantly would bother me.

I told my mother how the smell affected me and she dismissed my concern. I felt my mother wanted me to get married, and to me marriage seemed preferable to living where I felt I wasn't really wanted. Since my mother knew Harold wanted to marry me, she told him she'd give him moral support. "Gwennie, you get on that side and hold him and I'll hold him on this side, and that'll give him courage to ask your father's permission to marry you."

Mother called to Daddy and told him to sit down, and then we three sat on the couch together across from Daddy. "Herb, Harold has something he wants to ask you," my mother told my dad.

Harold started off by saying, "I know you have plenty of reasons to tell me, no, but I want to marry your daughter and I want your permission."

My dad got choked up. "Well, Gwennie's the only daughter I have, and if you were to live right around here where I could see her it would be one thing, but you're planing to live in California. Do you expect to take her way out there so we can't see her anymore?"

"I know it would be a long way off, but I promise to bring her back to visit you once each year. There's so much more money to be made in California and that's where I want to settle."

I could see that Daddy wasn't sure he wanted to let me go, but Mother finally convinced him it was the right thing to do.

Harold was all fired up about getting my parents' permission to marry me that I wonder if I ever told him, "Yes," because I was still thinking about what it would mean to go that far away with someone I barely knew.

Though I don't recall when I said yes, we went to pick out an engagement ring. I felt like it should have been an exciting time but it wasn't. I knew Harold didn't have that much money so I picked out a very lovely ring that had a modest-sized diamond. I could see the prices and I picked a set with an engagement and wedding ring that fit together that cost about one hundred dollars, which seemed plenty for Harold to have to pay.

I wonder now why the fact Harold wasn't a Christian didn't send up red flags. I know now that Christians and non-Christians don't have the most important thing in life in common—their faith. My mother talked to

Harold about God and was convinced he believed there was a God. I know now, that wasn't enough. For Christians to be able to communicate about their faith, it is necessary that they receive Jesus as their Savior and make Him Lord over their life.

Do not be yoked together with unbelievers....What does a believer have in common with an unbeliever? (2 Corinthians 6:14 a-15b).

✿ Our Honeymoon to San Francisco

On September 28, 1946, Harold came again from California, and this time we had made plans to be married in the St. Paul Lutheran Church, where I had been confirmed. Pastor Jesse had moved on to become part of the governing body of the Missouri Synod Lutheran Church. The new pastor, Pastor Brauer, talked to Harold and me before he married us.

My mother, father, and baby brother were the only ones attending our wedding on September 29, 1946. Harold had said he wanted as small a wedding as possible. My folks didn't really have the money to give me a big wedding and I had paid for my suit, which I could wear after the wedding. I bought material and sewed my night gowns, and bought the rest of my clothes for the trip, spending almost all of the money I had. We left St. Joseph, Missouri the evening we were married and headed for San Francisco, California.

This was during the time when rubber was scarce and tires were hard to buy. We had one flat after another. We were stopping quite frequently to have tires patched.

At last we had time to get better acquainted, though the marriage wasn't consummated until the second evening of our honeymoon, because we were both inexperienced. Most of the couples I knew in the forties, waited until after the wedding before becoming physically involved and marriages lasted longer than they do today.

Our honeymoon trip took seven days. By the time we arrived in San Francisco, we were two young people very much in love. My Aunt Marie later teased me about a postcard I wrote her on my honeymoon. It read, "Harold is five foot eight and I love every inch of him."

Since we arrived in San Francisco with only the ten dollars my grandfather gave us for a wedding gift, it's a good thing I ate hamburgers along the way. Harold ordered cheeseburgers, but I knew our money situation and neither of us had a credit card. So I ate conservatively hoping we'd have enough money to make it to California. Harold's paycheck was waiting for him when we got to San Francisco.

I loved San Francisco from the moment I first glimpsed it from the Bay Bridge. Everyone in St. Joseph had told me how dirty and foggy it was, I didn't think we'd be able to see. In Missouri we had the kind of fog where you couldn't see ten feet in front of you. When we drove across the bridge and I saw that picturesque town set on those beautiful hills basking under a sunny sky, I was thrilled. The houses were white and clean and I couldn't figure out what people were talking about when they said it was dirty. I have to admit there were a few streets that I saw later that weren't as clean as they might have been, but I always felt fortunate to have been able to live in such a beautiful city for thirteen years.

I loved the climate. During the first winter, I didn't even wear a coat and I couldn't understand why people were cold. After a couple of years I became acclimated and I felt the colder weather in winter and sometimes even in the cooler summer months when the fog rolled in, too.

We had a real problem finding a place to live, because we arrived at the end of the war when there was a real shortage of rentals. We moved in with Harold's father and mother until we found a place of our own.

We were very excited to get an apartment on the third floor in an old house with a winding staircase, that had survived the 1906 San Francisco earthquake. It still had gas lights that had been used at one time. We had two rooms; quite a large kitchen with a step-up bath and wash room and then on the other side of the stairs was our bedroom. It wasn't much to look at but it was home to us. The rent was thirty-five dollars a month. For fun we often spent twenty-five cents and bought a book to read together in bed. When salaries are one hundred and fifty dollars a month you can't afford movies and television. Although we attended the movies rarely, I don't believe television had actually come on the market when we married. It may have already been invented, but TV's weren't in the average home yet.

One day someone rang the doorbell and I looked out the upstairs window. The person below called out, "Your roof is on fire!"

Thinking someone was playing a prank, I said, "Sure it is." Then I heard the fire trucks coming up the hill and I ran down the stairs looking for Minnie, the elderly woman who lived there, but I couldn't find her so I ran out of the building allowing the door to lock behind me.

Gwen Lawan Johnson

By the time the firemen finished chopping out the roof, they'd made a mess out of our apartment and we were out of a place to live. Our apartment had been condemned because there was no fire escape from the third floor. The nice folks who rented it to us gave us another apartment down the street on the first floor. We made the room you walked into, a living room which served as a bedroom when the couch folded out at night. We had a large kitchen with a little porch and the bath on the back of the house.

We bought little things like frilly curtains to give our apartment a homey look, but they didn't cost much.

Buying another car was a big purchase. The car we drove out to California was the same car Harold fell asleep in when driving back to see me. Thank God there were metal barriers to stop him from hurtling into a mountain ravine. However, the impact of the collision left the car with a set of permanently waved fenders. People always stopped for us, because if we got hit no one would have known the difference, but we looked as if we could inflict a lot of damage on another car.

This car after a number of trips between California and Missouri finally became completely worn out. Harold had the chance to buy a '37 Cadillac in mint condition for five hundred dollars and he did. It got only nine miles per gallon, but what a beauty it was all loaded with chrome against a deep forest green, with the most gorgeous upholstery and a luxurious arm rest that pulled down in back. People always said, "It's a good thing your husband works where he can buy gas." Several years later we sold that car for seven hundred and fifty dollars.

One place I loved to visit in San Francisco was St. Francis Woods where the beautiful mansions are. Each home displays a completely different type of architecture with a picturesque yard, landscaped and groomed impeccably. I saw them again recently and they are still just as lovely as they were in 1946.

Going to the top of twin peaks and looking down at San Francisco always took my breath away.

I can never get enough of Golden Gate Park when the flowers are in bloom; especially the rhododendrons and azaleas. I love the aquarium, and going through the Japanese Tea Gardens. Coit Tower was another place we loved to take our guests.

Of course, all the tourists go to Fisherman's Wharf, China Town, and the wonderful zoo. I can remember when there was Playland at the beach, when a funny looking lady stood up high in a window and laughed as we went by.

Wanted by God

The undeveloped McLaren Park which covered quite an expanse of land, extended to the hills across the street from our first real home. This park was named after the man who designed the Golden Gate Park. Now the McLaren Park has been developed and it is lovely. It includes a golf course.

One morning I awakened and thought I was dreaming. I looked out our bedroom window and there were snow-covered hills across the street. It wasn't a dream! It was the only time I can remember it snowing enough in San Francisco to actually cover the ground.

It was a great place to live, and I'm very happy Harold brought me to such a beautiful city.

He has made everything beautiful in its time. He has also set eternity in the hearts of men; yet they cannot fathom what God had done from beginning to end (Ecclesiastes 3:11).

4
God's Blessings—Home, Church, and Family

But from everlasting to everlasting the Lord's love is with those who fear him, and his righteousness with their children's children—with those who keep his covenant and remember to obey his precepts (Psalm 103:17,18).

 Welcoming Our Daughter

 A New Home Near Church

 Prayer Answered While Praying on My Knees

How great is the love the Father has lavished on us, that we should be called children of God!... and what we will be has not yet been made known. But we know that when he appears we shall be like him for we shall see him as he is (1 John 3:1,2).

❀ Welcoming Our Daughter

I awoke with labor pains. It was Sunday, so I asked Harold, "What could we do better than to attend church on our baby's birthday?" This time my husband decided he'd better go to church with me. During the service my pains were about fifteen minutes apart. When we came out we decided to go to Harold's parents' home because they lived closer to the hospital.

Harold's mother was so upset by my being in labor she paced the floor. I think she was afraid I'd have the baby right there. While they were trying to figure out what to do with me I prepared lunch for the three of us. You see, my labor was almost a month early. The doctor had figured December 20th to be my due date, and it was only November 30th. Finally the labor pains were closer to five minutes apart and the doctor said, "Come to the hospital now and I'll meet you there."

When I got to the hospital I said, "I don't think I'm ready to have a baby; it doesn't hurt bad enough." The nurse said, "Look at your abdomen." I did. It heaved up and down like ten foot waves. "Now, tell me you're not ready to have a baby. You're fully dilated, and we're getting you to the delivery room as fast as possible."

My mother-in-law had left to go have a cup of coffee because I was sure it would be some time before the birth.

They got me on the delivery table and I gave birth. I never even thought of screaming.

"She's a healthy baby girl," the doctor announced, as he showed me my unwashed baby. She gave a howl and I knew she had good lungs.

The nurse said, "We'll clean her up and you can see her at nursing time."

They wheeled me into another little room and sent my mother-in-law there when she came back from having a cup of coffee. She sat down and started to visit, talking about how much longer it would be before the baby would come.

"Oh no, Mother, the baby is already here. She's a sweet little girl."

"You had a baby while I had a cup of coffee?" my mother-in-law stared at me as if she couldn't believe her ears.

"Well, Mom, I guess God allowed me an easy birth because of all the problems I had carrying her. Remember when they put me in the hospital to keep me from losing her? When I couldn't hold any food down they fed me through the veins. After all, I lost weight carrying little Teresa. Maybe now that she is here I can put a little weight back on. I sure won't miss vomiting every day."

"I guess you did get your problems out of the way so you could have an easy delivery," my mother-in-law agreed. "So you decided to name her Teresa. What's her middle name going to be?"

"Louise. She's Teresa Louise and we'll call her Terry Lou. Oh, Mom, God has been so good to me. I got through the birth so easily and I was supposed to go another three weeks. What a wonderful surprise to have had her early. I think that day I ran a block for the bus must have hurried her along. What day is this anyway?"

"November 30, 1947."

"So, that's little Terry's birthday, November 30th."

Harold walked into the room beaming. "Mom, you're back! Come down the hall and see our little Terry Lou. She looked long and thin and all hands and feet, before they wrapped her up in blankets. And has she got a pair of lungs!"

"Why don't you stay with Gwen and I'll go down and see her," Mother said.

"That wasn't too bad was it? I can't believe she's already here. Just think, I'm an eighteen-year-old mom and you're a twenty-three-year-old dad. How does it feel to be a father?"

"Oh, I guess I'll get used to it," Harold said grinning.

"I want to call Pastor Wallschlaeger and let him know our daughter's here." When I called our pastor to tell him I'd given birth he said, "Weren't you just at church this morning?"

"Yes, I was, and Harold was timing my labor pains all through the service. I thought that was a good way for our baby to start life by going to church on her birthday. She was born this evening and weighed six pounds eleven ounces.

"Her name is Teresa Louise and her nickname is Terry Lou."

I felt elated. A new baby daughter and I'd kept my vow not to scream. And I didn't have to miss church, either. Our Teresa Louise had all her fingers and toes and was a beautiful, healthy, and perfectly normal baby.

For you created my inmost being; you knit me together in my mother's womb (Psalm 139:13).

❀ A New Home Near Church

"Have you seen the new homes being built near here?" a friend asked me at church one Sunday.

"Exactly where are they building them?" I couldn't believe they were within a mile of the church. Harold and I went to look at the houses after he picked me up from church the next Sunday. When we found them, we could see they were within walking distance from the church I attended.

The homes cost $9,850 with only $500 down. We were excited. It seemed unbelievable but we could afford to buy one of these homes. If I hadn't heard about them at church we probably would never have seen them because we'd never driven to this area before. We didn't get the paper and we would have missed seeing these places we could afford. We put a down payment on one home that they were just beginning to build in order to have time to save money to buy furniture for our new house.

Our home was on a hill with a 10 percent grade, but we were young and could make it up the hill with no problem. We didn't have to worry about it sliding down the hill or washing away because three houses were built right next to us holding us up. Each house was built higher than the one next to it like stair steps, so yards were on different levels.

The undeveloped McLaren Park was across the street. There was a horse stable, full of horses and goats roamed the hills. Every morning a rooster crowed about 5:30 a.m. People had leased the land for their animals. A family also leased out the one house across the street until the park was developed. Barbara, who later became a friend of my daughter, lived there. The setting was lovely. It was like living in the country but getting to downtown San Francisco by bus in about twenty minutes on the freeway.

"Honey, isn't it exciting? We own a house of our own and we have a great big yard for Terry to play in." Harold was excited, too. He just contained his excitement more. The house wasn't large, like the new homes of today, but it was extremely comfortable with two bedrooms. It was only 850 square feet and had a basement. We often took a drive to see how fast it was going up. Naturally it took longer to build than we'd hoped, but it did give us time to save money to buy furniture and all of the things necessary to set up housekeeping in our own home.

Inexpensive houses are wonderful for young couples. It's a great way to build equity for a larger home later. Why doesn't some builder build smaller homes for young people today so that they don't have to pay half their salary for a home?

The Lutheran church I'd been attending was about six blocks away. I had gone alone to church for over eleven years and I never quit praying that Harold would become a Christian. After much pleading, Harold enrolled in a class to find out more about the Bible and the Christian faith. The class was supposed to end in six weeks but went on fourteen or fifteen weeks because Harold challenged everything. He had some good arguments. Finally the pastor convinced him that God's way was the right way and he decided he'd be baptized and join the church. Baptism is the one thing he had said no one would ever get him to do. I think the Holy Spirit prevailed. The pastor told me that Harold's conversion was the most pleasing to him of all the people he had ever taught, because he was such a challenge.

The night he was accepted as a member he was also elected to be an elder. He really loved the older pastor who had stuck with him and taught him the Bible was true.

After about eight years our elderly pastor's wife died and he retired and went to live nearer his relatives. The church body filled in with interim pastors and finally decided on Pastor Carl Wallis and sent him a call.

Having Harold in church with me was certainly an answer to eleven years of steady praying. I wanted a husband that believed in the Lord Jesus as his Savior and Harold did, but at this time neither of us had made Him Lord over our lives.

Our next door neighbor mentioned how different Harold was since he'd started attending church. I knew it was certainly better for Terry to have both parents believing in God and attending church together. Since we were united in our faith we could give Terry a more stable upbringing.

I had wanted another child, but I suffered a miscarriage when Terry was five. Nevertheless, I was still praying God would bless us with another child.

God was teaching me to have faith and to be patient. He'd blessed us with a new home and we were busy designing a large yard because our lot was one hundred and twenty feet deep. The back thirty-five feet was to be a playground for whatever children we would have.

God had already answered so many prayers. Harold was not only a member of our church but an active one. Now we'd been able to purchase our own home, and while we were waiting for it to finish being built we'd been able to shop and buy enough furniture to create a lovely interior for our brand new home.

Devote yourselves to prayer, being watchful and thankful (Colossians 4:2).

❀ Prayer Answered While Praying on My Knees

Our new Pastor Wallis and his wife Gloria became our two closest friends. Their daughter Annette, was Terry's age and their son Kirk, several years younger. Our two families got together nearly every Sunday afternoon. We'd pool what food we had and come out with something delicious.

During this time I found out I was pregnant. We'd wanted another baby. I'd had one miscarriage and things didn't look too good this time, either. I had a prolapsed uterus and it was tipped over with the baby inside. My gynecologist said if it didn't upright itself soon, my baby could die.

During this very difficult time I was down on my knees praying, "Dear heavenly Father, please let me carry this baby full term. You know how much we wanted another child. It was so difficult losing that baby three years ago. Terry is almost eight, Lord, and You know how hard it is for me to get pregnant. Heavenly Father, please protect my child and allow me to carry this fetus full term. Thank You, Lord, for all of your many blessings and help me to accept your will in this matter, Amen."

Suddenly I had a terrible pain in my lower abdomen. "Oh no, Lord, I just can't be losing this baby, too. I don't think I could bear it."

I rushed to the phone and called my obstetrician. The nurse who answered the phone spoke to my doctor and he said I should get there as soon as possible. We had only one car and Harold had driven it to work, and besides I couldn't drive anyway even if we had another car. I hadn't been allowed to drive because Harold said I was not mechanical enough to handle a car.

I decided to call and see if Mrs. Jackson next door could drive me. She knew how much I wanted this baby. I put a call through to her and she answered.

Wanted by God

"Mrs. Jackson, I've just had some very sharp pains and my doctor wants me to come in right away. Could you drive me? Bless your heart. Thank you. I'll be right over."

When I arrived the doctor saw me at once. He knew my pregnancy had been difficult with vomiting every day and some hemorrhaging, too. But what worried him most was my tipped uterus. He hadn't wanted to force it up because it might injure the baby.

The nurse prepared me to see the doctor and he came in. "You had some abdominal pain this morning?" he asked.

"I was on my knees praying, and all of a sudden I had sharp pains and something happened. It's hard to explain."

"Well, what happened is your prayer worked. What we wanted to happen, has taken place. The pain you felt was your uterus coming into an upright position. It would hurt because it's been stuck in that precarious position for three months now. Our worries are over for now. I still want you to go straight to bed when there is any sign of blood. All right?"

"Is the baby out of danger now?"

"Yes. Your uterus is in the normal position now. There is no longer any chance of the child aborting because of a tipped uterus."

Inwardly I breathed, *Thank You, God. You heard me and answered my prayer. I think my kneeling to pray helped to tip my uterus upright. You are good to me, Lord.*

I couldn't wait to tell Mrs. Jackson the good news. My prayer had been answered. My baby was safe.

Six months later I gave birth to a six pound, five ounce baby girl. Terry had a sister, Cynthia Marie, whom we called Cindy May. Cindy was such a good baby and slept so much, sometimes I had to awaken her just to talk to her. What a blessing she was for all of us.

God has surely listened and heard my voice in prayer (Psalm 66:19).

5

God's Presence Opens Me to His Service

You have made known to me the path of life;
you will fill me with joy in your presence,
with eternal pleasures at your right hand
(Psalm 16:11).

 In God's Presence

 The Truth about Suffering

 A Work of Love

 An Exciting League for Teenagers

I know you can do all things; no plan of yours can be
thwarted (Job 42:2).

❀ In God's Presence

After Cindy's birth the back pain was hurting worse than it ever had, and at times I even had trouble walking because of the pain. I consulted an internist who had an excellent reputation and who was highly recommended. His diagnosis was that I had a ruptured disc. He referred me to see one of the top neurosurgeons in San Francisco, who agreed with his diagnosis. He felt they needed to find the exact area of injury to see if surgery was advisable. This was the day I would get the dreaded myelogram I'd heard so much about. I had steeled myself trying to get ready for it.

The procedure was about to begin.

"You will be awake for this, Gwen," my tall athletic-looking doctor told me. "Your spine has already been deadened for the entrance of the needle. We will be injecting a radioactive solution which will highlight and detect problem areas. The table under you will be tilted in various angles so that the movement of the solution may be recorded on pictures known as myelograms." Dr. Webb continued to give directions to the technicians and then he told me to let them know if I became too uncomfortable.

"At times you will be nearly standing on your head, during the procedure, Gwen. We will not leave you in any position longer than necessary."

Inwardly I was thinking, *Please just get it over with.* I added a little prayer asking God to help me through the procedure.

"I feel faint," I heard my doctor say. "I cannot continue."

What is this—a soap opera? Was I a part of the drama for today? I couldn't believe my ears.

A hush fell over those in the room. One of the technicians reached out to help my doctor from the room. The needle was removed from my spine and nurses moved me from the table on to a portable bed and took me to a very small room and left me.

Would I have to return home without knowing the cause of my back pain after waiting all this time?

At times the intermittent back pains became excruciating ever since the bike accident at fifteen.

"I thought you were a goner," I had been told by a bystander who had witnessed the speeding automobile hit my bicycle, and who had seen me hurtled through the air.

Why had God spared me? And why had Dr. Webb been unable to complete the myelogram? My mind surged with questions. Someone was coming—maybe they'd know.

An invisible Presence filled my room. I felt an ecstatic peace and joy beyond human description as unseen arms enfolded me. God spoke—not audibly, but inwardly. The message penetrated my mind and heart. *"Don't be afraid, for I am with you. Don't be discouraged. I will strengthen you, and I will help you. I will hold you up with my victorious right hand."*

I repeated the message over and over in my mind. I didn't want to forget it or the peace and joy I'd known while the Presence of God was with me in my room. I knew God was always with me, but this was different—this time I felt visited by God.

A little later that day I was wheeled to my regular room.

That evening the hospital was buzzing about the doctor who nearly fainted when he was almost ready to start a myelogram.

Several days afterward, Dr. Webb finally completed the myelogram. "I'd had a bad case of the Asian flu," he explained. "I guess I tried to get back to my busy schedule too soon. I didn't want your spine filled with radioactive fluid and then I'd faint with you upside down on the table. I thought it was better to stop so that couldn't happen." He explained that if he was to perform surgery he wanted to see the myelogram so he'd know exactly where the problem was.

Several months later, Dr. Webb performed a laminectomy, during which he removed a ruptured disc in the right lower lumbar region.

On the day following surgery Pastor Wallis came to visit me. I was sitting up in bed, with my make-up on looking bright and cheerful. "You didn't have your surgery yet; what happened?" he asked.

"I did have my surgery yesterday," I told him.

A few minutes later an intern making his daily rounds came by and said, "I thought you were scheduled for back surgery yesterday. Why didn't they operate?"

"They did," I answered.

"Patients don't look like you do the day after back surgery," the intern said.

"This one does!" I replied, laughing.

"Come on, show me where they operated," he answered.

"Sorry, both of you will have to take my word for it. I had surgery yesterday."

When I am going through a big ordeal like surgery, it is very easy for me to hand it to Jesus and say, "You take it, Lord," and then relax and leave it with Him. For this reason, I come through surgery as if nothing happened, feeling fine. It's those little things I try to handle by myself because I don't want to bother Jesus with them, that really get me down.

I recovered so quickly I was sent home on the fifth day. I started cooking and cleaning and doing all my regular work, I felt so good. Then one day while I was putting clothes in our dryer, sharp pains hit my lower back. I became bent over and couldn't straighten up. I crawled back upstairs since our washer and dryer were in the basement.

One spasm set off another one and soon my back, right leg, and arm were all going into spasm. Finally, I was unable to move in bed because of the severe spasms. It became too difficult for me to be cared for at home. My husband called an ambulance to take me back to the hospital. The ambulance attendants put me on a stretcher to carry me down the stairs. My body slipped. A piercing scream echoed in the hall stairs caused by the most intense pain I ever felt as spasms struck throughout my entire body.

During the next five years I suffered with back spasms. "You're having spasms like a polio victim," the physical therapist told me. During those years, I returned to the hospital four times for therapy and tests. I couldn't move without muscle spasms.

While confined to my bed I read the Bible. One day I was reading my Bible in the book of Isaiah, a book I hadn't remembered reading before. The words sounded very familiar. "*Do not fear, for I am with you; do not be dismayed, for I am your God. I will strengthen you and help you; I will uphold you with my righteous right hand*" (Isaiah 41:10).

This message was almost exactly the same as the one I'd received in that little hospital room while I waited to see when I'd be rescheduled for a myelogram.

This promise was a beautiful one to lean on during years of pain that would have been impossible without the love of almighty God, the comfort of the Holy Spirit and the knowledge that eternal life was mine through Jesus Christ my Lord. I'd never forget those words during the difficult days ahead. There were times I wondered if I would ever walk again. I prayed, "If this is Your will for me not to walk, I'll accept it." My back slowly started to improve.

Be strong and take heart all you who hope in the Lord (Psalm 31:24).

❀ The Truth about Suffering

Many people say a good God wouldn't allow suffering.

In my life I've been diagnosed as deaf, blind, and lame and I've endured more than a dozen surgeries and I would still ask, "Why should we be surprised that suffering is a part of our lives?" We might not know why we suffer but God knows.

God certainly loved Jesus, and He still allowed Him to suffer. He wasn't punishing Jesus because of sin, since He never sinned. On the cross Jesus suffered what He didn't deserve so we could have what we don't deserve. Because we all have sinned we deserve death, but through faith in Jesus, we have the promise of everlasting life. There were moments on the cross when Jesus felt completely forsaken by His Father, God, because of our sin which separated Him from His Father. Yet He willingly agreed to suffer such agony for you and for me. The Bible tells us that Jesus *Who for the joy set before him endured the cross* (Hebrew 12:2). His joy would be sitting on the throne at the right hand of His Father, and knowing the believers who would inherit eternal life, because of His sacrifice.

We sometimes have a cross to bear because of the joy set before us; the joy of seeing our husband, children, or friends who, without our cross, might never have received Jesus as their Lord and Savior. This is the mystery of suffering according to God's will.

Suffering is our teacher. It teaches us compassion for others and gives us insight. Since I have suffered it helps me to be able to identify with and minister to others who are suffering. Suffering strengthens faith in God. However, suffering may weaken the faith of those whose belief was already deficient in the beginning. Suffering has taught me to trust God in all situations. Suffering from misfortune, trials, and pain does not mean God has forsaken those He loves. He has reasons we know nothing about. Unless He chooses to reveal them to us in His own time, we must simply trust Him.

Job never received an answer for his terrible suffering. However, his personal confrontation with God not only silenced his arguing, it showed him how full of pride he had been to insist that God answer him. He repented in dust and ashes. Job gained a completely new perspective of God through the loss of his family and his health. He had a much higher regard for God after God questioned him. He stood in awe of God's majesty and power. "*Surely, I spoke of things I did not understand,*" he confessed, "*things too wonderful for me to know.... My ears had heard of you but now my eyes have seen you"* (Job 42:3,5). Suffering helped Job to comprehend God's authority over all things. After Job confessed his pride and repented, God restored his estate with twice the amount he'd had before. Job fathered ten more children and he lived to see his great great grandchildren by living to the ripe old age of two hundred and ten.

The book of Job is a good thing to read when we're suffering. Job's three friends were rebuked by God. Instead of praying for their friend, they insisted Job was suffering because of some sin in his life. God exonerated Job. Though Job contended with God, he never renounced Him, as Satan had said he would.

After Job's acknowledgment of the truth, God praised him, restored his health and told Job's friends to have Job pray for them. God told them to offer burnt sacrifices to Him because they had not told the truth like His servant Job had.

Each of us can expect some form of struggle while we search for God's purpose for our lives. Even after we receive Jesus, there will be difficulties, but with Jesus' Spirit living in us, we experience God's peace and contentment even in life's worst storms.

God knew before my birth I would suffer a great deal of pain, both physical and mental. He knew that through this pain I would have a deeper understanding of Him and His will for my life and that I would become His servant. However, before this could take place, my strong "self-will" had to be broken. Brokenness was a matter of surrendering control to God in the same way a horse that has been broken becomes sensitive to what its master wants. Once my heart was emptied of my self-will and broken so I would be sensitive to God's leading, He could teach me His will.

A seed cannot grow unless it falls into the ground and breaks open to send forth a new plant. A baby chick cannot be hatched until it breaks open the shell from the inside to crawl out. If someone on the outside breaks the shell, the little chick is weakened and will probably not survive. It is life's struggles that make us strong and valuable to God and to others who are facing trials.

When our "self-will" is broken, a new creation in Christ steps forward, a willing servant. We are the same person with the same individuality and the same characteristics, only now we use them for God's purpose in place of our own. Finding God's purpose for our life fills us with great joy and fulfills us in a way we never thought possible. Writing has been one of the ways God has fulfilled me.

My life could have been easier, but I would never ask for ease if it meant giving up the relationship I enjoy with God today. I became a partner in Christ's suffering. By suffering with Him, I will also reign with Him and share His glory.

Rejoice that you participate in the sufferings of Christ, so you may be overjoyed when his glory is revealed (1 Peter 4:13). Those who accept a wheelchair, crutches or braces with joy, and serve and honor Christ in a praiseworthy manner, will one day share Christ's glory.

Joni Eareckson Tada, confined to a wheelchair for more than three decades after a swimming accident left her paralyzed as a teenager, is a perfect example of a person filled with the joy of the Lord. Her writing has influenced many people.

Joni's book, *Heaven, Your Real Home*, tells of her happy expectations of heaven. Her descriptions of heaven capture my imagination like no other. I have prepared myself for the joys of heaven. My having a glorified body that will never suffer pain again, makes me look forward to the day God calls me home to be with Him. I won't only have a glorified body and mind, I'll have a purified heart that thinks only of those things that are true, pure, excellent, and praiseworthy.

We who believe in Jesus, will be lifted up from death to eternal life in wonderful glorified bodies like Jesus had when He appeared in the midst of the disciples. Just think of all the places we will be able to go where no man has gone before.

When suffering comes, think of it as God reaching out in love to refine and purify our lives, by making those He loves ready for the joys of His heavenly Kingdom.

Our citizenship is in heaven. And we eagerly await a Savior from there, the Lord Jesus Christ, who, by the power that enables him to bring everything under his control, will transform our lowly bodies so that they will be like his glorious body (Philippians 3:20-21).

❀ A Work of Love

Harold had been elected the president of the Board of Elders, and he'd taken over as Sunday School Superintendent. One night he brought the Sunday School files home to bring them up to date.

In looking over the Sunday School attendance cards I learned that forty-five young people who attended our Sunday School had not been baptized. I visited their homes and spoke with them and their parents and they were all ready and willing to become baptized. An afternoon service of baptisms took place one Sunday afternoon. All forty-five children I'd visited were baptized. I was the sponsor for three of them. I praised God for using me in this way.

Pastor Ellerman, the interim pastor, asked me a strange question.

"Gwen, you went personally and got all of these children for baptism and you work with our Senior League and you teach Sunday School. What does your house look like? Does your furniture have an inch of dust piled up? I don't know how you do all these things, raise two children and keep a home, too."

"I do all of these things because I love God, and I want to help others to have eternal life in Christ Jesus. I also want them to experience the joy that comes from knowing Jesus as their Savior," I told him.

At that time Jesus came from Nazareth in Galilee and was baptized by John in the Jordan. As Jesus was coming up out of the water, he saw heaven being torn open and the Spirit descending on him like a dove. And a voice came from heaven: "You are my Son, whom I love; with you I am well pleased" (Mark 1: 9-11).

❀ An Exciting League for Teenagers

One night Harold came home from church saying that they were going to drop the Walther League for the older kids. "I think it should continue even though Pastor and I met with the three members that are left and they said, "Let it drop." They told us they really didn't want a league. "But, what about all the other young people who might really benefit from having a Christ-centered organization?" he asked me.

I had been a teenager who had benefited from a Walther League. "I remember how I loved the times spent with other kids from church. We had good times without drinking, taking drugs, or getting caught up in sex. I have to admit I would have lost out on many good times if our church hadn't had a Walther League."

"Gwen, what do you think about us taking it over?" Harold asked me.

"We'd be leaving Terry and Cindy at home with a baby sitter in order to be counselors to some kids who don't care about the league. Does that make good sense?"

I prayed about it and I thought about it more and I was giving in. Harold was willing to take on another job in addition to being the Sunday School Superintendent, and the president of the Board of Elders in the church. First I couldn't get him to church and now he practically lived there. He'd become so embroiled in jobs at church it seemed he spent more time there than at home.

In 1959 we became the counselors of the Senior Walther League. By 1962 we had fifty-two members and at one of the outings eighty-eight teenagers attended. It was perfect for me. I was so young that I fit right in with the kids and I got to attend all the outings with them. It was fun for me to go roller skating, swimming, to play table tennis, hike, bike ride, go on hay rides and all sorts of outings. I had a real rapport with teenagers. They treated me just like I was one of them.

We hired sitters for our two daughters so we would have evenings free for a business meeting to plan our programs and our outings which generally took place on the weekend. To earn money for service projects, the teenagers washed cars on Saturday. The league actually paid for the twenty-four foot lighted aluminum cross on the front of our new church, by having car washes, selling Christmas cards, and dried fruit gifts and by giving bake sales to earn money for the cross project.

I loved every one of those teenagers and they loved me. I provided unconditional love and nurturing and Harold provided them with the discipline they needed. We made sure they had devotions prepared ahead of time and a topic to talk over with the group every month. All the kids actually did their own devotions and topics and they made them beautiful and interesting. No one ever missed preparing. They felt it was an honor to do the topic and they made it something worthwhile. Sometimes the devotions were so moving, I cried. Those teenagers knew their Lord and Savior and they weren't ashamed to let everyone else know it. I felt we were making a real impact on these teenagers and their parents thanked us for what we were doing. Parents were happy to help out when we had progressive dinners or to drive a carload of kids when we had outings. We had wonderful cooperation from parents because they approved of what we were doing for their teenagers.

My life was full. And I had never been happier!

The league had a monthly newspaper giving the times and places for all the activities. The first thing they read was "Dirt by Gert," a favorite with all of the teens. No one knew who wrote it but me, since I got all the juicy tidbits from other leaguers or from their moms and dads.

"How does this person know all these things?" they'd ask.

I had scads of fun writing that column and no one ever guessed it was me. They were dumbfounded when I finally told them I had written the column, after we were transferred to Santa Cruz. As close as I was to those kids I was amazed they hadn't guessed it was me. I think they felt only a teenager could have written it. To know the things I wrote, I had to be right in the center of their activities and I was.

I was at every car wash, bake sale and whatever method we used to gain money to pay for the lighted cross on the front of the church. I was the adult who accompanied the teens on their outings. Harold also attended beach parties and walked along with them to the homes of various leaguers for progressive dinners. One course was served at each home, including: hors d'oeuvres, soup, salad, a main dish, and finally dessert. One night we had a backward progressive dinner. Some of the kids even wore their clothes backwards. We started with dessert and ended with hors d'oeuvres.

One place we liked to go in warm weather had an outdoor pool where we could also play Ping-Pong and volleyball and I was right there playing with them. One funny incident happened when we went to a skating rink. I was around twenty-three and all these sixteen and eighteen year olds were calling me Mom. They had other skaters asking, "She's not really your mom, is she?" All of them insisted I was their mom. One man who asked me to skate in a couples skate was really confused because he couldn't figure out how that was possible. "You're not old enough to have had one of these kids let alone twenty-five," he told me.

They started calling me "Mom" or "Mommie" when Cindy came to bring messages to our Sunday School class. She called me "Mommie" so they just all started calling me that, too.

When new members entered the league after they were confirmed, we held a big initiation party in the club house at Sigmond Stern Grove. We hired a square dance caller, who the teens really loved. Sarah called the square dances after the initiation stunts were over. It was a fantastic way for the younger members, who were coming into the league, to mix with the older members and really get to know them. Square dancing proved to be a great way to unite the different age groups.

Wanted by God

A quiet prayer time followed the rollicking dance time, to prepare the teens for a quiet ride home. One of the members of the league started a silent time at the end of a business meeting held at the church, so we ended our outings with a prayer time, too. The kids dedicated a place to pray and they could decide whether they wanted to pray there or sitting in their seats. When the closing was in our church they went forward as they felt the Holy Spirit's leading to pray. They knelt at the kneeling rail at the front of the church and stayed in prayer as long as they wished. They liked it so much they ended all their business meetings, after topic and devotions, and now their fun outings, too, with a prayer time.

Being a counselor for this league was one of the most worthwhile and enjoyable things I've done. The growth of the kids was amazing. The last news I heard from San Francisco was that three of the young men from our group were studying to become ministers.

During the years we served as counselors at Grace Lutheran Church in San Francisco, the church took a poll of all the members who attended church and they found the fifteen to nineteen-year-old boys attended the most often and the fifteen to nineteen-year-old girls were the second best age group in attendance.

I taught the teenage Sunday School Group and we had over thirty in attendance every week. When the pastor entered the hospital for surgery the adult class joined our teenage group. Two members enjoyed it so much, they often came back to visit our class and the teenagers didn't seem to mind.

After more than six years as counselors, my husband's job transferred him to Santa Cruz and one of the boys quipped, "We may be losing counselors but we're gaining a resort." Santa Cruz is known for its beaches and surfing.

This same young man who had seen me downstairs weeping because we had to leave these wonderful young people, told the others: "Gwen's downstairs having a bawl."

Almost weekly, kids came to Santa Cruz to spend time with us over the weekend. Then they came monthly and finally we saw them occasionally. I loved them for wanting to be with us. Finally some married and had children of their own. They wrote me letters and sent pictures of their little ones. We had become family.

Accept one another, then, just as Christ accepted you, in order to bring praise to God (Romans 15:7).

6

Unexpected Surprises: Happy and Sorrowful

And the God of all grace, who called you to his eternal glory in Christ, after you have suffered a little while, will himself restore you and make you strong, firm and steadfast (1 Peter 5:10).

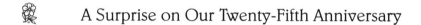 A Surprise on Our Twenty-Fifth Anniversary

Mom's Stroke Reunites the Family

Creativity Stimulated through Illness

Mother's Death—A Time of Reflection

A Testing of Faith

Just as man is destined to die once, and after that to face judgement; so Christ was sacrificed once to take away the sins of many people; and he will appear a second time, not to bear sin, but to bring salvation to those who are waiting for him (Hebrews 9:27-28).

❀ A Surprise on Our Twenty-Fifth Anniversary

We knew something unusual was about to take place when our sixteen-year-old daughter, Cindy, blindfolded her father and me and led us up the street from where we lived. We were told to step up, and then I could tell we went through two doorways and our blindfolds were taken off, and a group of people sitting around a table shouted, "Surprise!" Surprised we were!

Cindy had gathered Pastor Carl Wallis and his wife Gloria, from San Francisco; the Sheriff of Santa Cruz, Doug James and his wife Betty, who had lived across from us in Soquel; and Ann and Frank Phillips who had lived two doors from us in San Francisco, and remained our friends through their move back to Minnesota, and then back out to California again to live in Novato. No one could have any better or dearer friends than these three couples. In addition there was Alice, who worked with Cindy to help make a wonderful turkey dinner for us, and opened her home to make this an extra special day.

All of our friends got along famously though they hadn't met previous to this special festive time marking our twenty-five happy years of marriage. I believe both of us would have agreed that our marriage had been grand, full of love and filled with happiness. Seeing Pastor and Gloria was such a treat, and Betty and Doug had been our closest friends in Soquel. We'd known Ann and Frank from Novato for more than twenty years. Our party couldn't have been any more fun nor could the food have been any more delicious. I've never heard people laugh more or have as much fun as we all did that day.

Alice always added to a party, and Cindy stayed focused on seeing that we enjoyed ourselves, and we certainly did. How Cindy managed to do all the planning, shopping, and preparing such a large turkey dinner without even a hint of this celebration coming up was amazing. Any couple who lives together twenty-five happy years has a great deal to be thankful for. God had blessed our marriage and our work in the church, especially with the young people, and we had many friends in Aptos, Soquel and Santa Cruz.

If anyone had told me what would happen to our marriage in the future, I wouldn't have believed them.

Perfume and incense bring joy to the heart, and the pleasantness of one's friend[s] *springs from his earnest counsel* (Proverbs 27:9).

❀ Mom's Stroke Reunites the Family

My brother, Henry, went into the service when he was eighteen and I was sixteen, and that was the last time our immediate family had been together until my mother's stroke, when I was forty-six.

My eldest brother, Henry, met me at the Grand Junction, Colorado Airport. We had not corresponded or seen each other for years. Within the ride to our folks' house, I poured out that I was suffering great difficulties in my thirty-year marriage. To my surprise, Henry who had been divorced and happily remarried again, encouraged me to do everything I could to save my marriage. I'd thought if anyone would understand my situation it would be him.

At the house my younger brother, Ronnie, who was only three years old when I was married, seemed quite happy to see me. He missed home cooked meals. My being able to cook for our original family gave me a sense of well-being. After all these years I felt connected again.

I found Mother to be in much better condition than Daddy had described over the phone. The stroke had paralyzed Mother's right side, but with Daddy making her exercise and walk every half hour all day and part of the night, God had restored movement in all but her right hand. Since she had always been ambidextrous, she could use her left hand to do everything, including writing. My mother had written that they'd meet me half way when they moved to Grand Junction, Colorado from St. Joseph, Missouri. Ronnie had always lived at home with our parents, so we saw him when we took our trip back to visit.

Usually on about our third day back, Mother found fault with me or the way I raised Terry and Cindy. That hadn't happened this trip. I'd had a wonderful time. The stroke seemed to have deadened the "critical parent" part of Mom's brain that continually found fault with me. We sat side by side on her organ bench, and I helped push the fingers of her right hand on the keyboard hoping life would return in her hand. She'd play the soprano part and I played the bass chords. We played simple little melodies and it was fun when we played a hymn where we could recognize the tune. We laughed and laughed at some of our pitiful attempts to play old hymns, because they sounded completely out of harmony. Since Henry had arrived earlier than I had, he left soon after I came, giving Mother and me time alone together. I praise God for allowing this wonderful time with my mother so I could remember her this way. After our organ playing grew tiresome we decided to paint.

Although Mom had never attempted to paint until after sixty, she turned out some very fine paintings. However, she had started one painting that she had left unfinished because it wasn't turning out the way she'd hoped. We decided to paint over top of the old painting, since you can do that with oils. Together we turned her unfinished painting into a very lovely vase of daisies. This was positively the only time Mother and I ever painted together, and we really enjoyed each other's company. She didn't once correct me or tell me I couldn't do things right.

I had never witnessed the inner child in my mother before and it was a delight to watch her playful child come out and her "critical parent" disappear. I think the reason children love to be around me is because I have such a playful inner child. That inner child of mine helped draw my mother's inner child out to play.

This is a part of all of us that can have fun. My inner child gets me away from everyday stress so I can become wide-eyed and full of wonder and look at things with a real curiosity. Children are inquisitive, eager to learn, questioning, and always searching to find new things to be interested in. In fact that description sounds like my brother, Ronnie, too. *Could the reason we both enjoy our inner child so much, be because our inner child was the only part of us that could cope with feelings that we weren't what Mother wanted when we were born?* Ronnie often repeated that it was difficult to be told day after day a tough little boy wasn't exactly what your mother was looking for after the loss of a precious little girl like Gloria Joy.

I know my folks adored Ronnie, but each time Mom said, "Here we wanted a little girl to take Gloria's place and we got this tough looking little boy," Ronnie heard he wasn't really the child they wanted.

I feel sure my mother didn't say these things to hurt us. She was a good mother in many ways, especially in the way she pointed all three of us kids toward our Lord and Savior, Jesus Christ, for which I am eternally grateful. That's the best gift any parent can offer their child.

I have always been extremely happy that on this last visit with my mother, God left me with pleasant memories from start to finish of our having a great time together. I enjoyed my mother's company and she enjoyed mine. I also enjoyed our original family spending time together.

That was the last time all of us were alive as a family. I want to hold the memory of this trip forever in my mind.

Even in laughter the heart may ache, and the joy may end in grief (Proverbs 14:13).

🌸 Creativity Stimulated through Illness

Pneumonia had put me in bed. My doctor said, "I'm sending you to the hospital unless you promise to stay in bed." I'm a person who can't stand to be idle, except to pray.

Although I loved to paint it had been years since I'd picked up a brush. If I could prop myself up in bed I knew I could use this time to paint a watercolor. During the next two months, I spent nearly two hundred hours painting an involved snow scene reminding me of Missouri in the winter. This painting has always been my favorite of all the ones I've done.

Rarely do I have the time to spend painting. Any time I'm creating something, I'm happy because creativity brings me in touch with my heavenly Father. After all He is the greatest Creator of all. There is excitement in taking a blank piece of paper or an empty canvas and watch as a lovely painting results. I always know with the living God breathing His breath into my efforts, it will become something of value.

When we lived in Soquel near Santa Cruz, I entered an art contest. An artist was showing how to paint a watercolor using washes and I use almost a dry brush. I felt almost embarrassed because my technique appeared to be wrong. "Let's take my painting and go home," I whispered to my husband. We walked over to where my painting hung and there was a large white envelope attached. I opened the envelope and it stated, "You have won First Place in the Non Oil Division." One of the judges came over and asked, "What medium did you use? I couldn't decide if it was a water color or a pastel."

My using an almost dry brush created something different in water colors and it taught me that it pays to be different. We don't all have to do things exactly in the same manner as someone else. We need to be individuals who allow our Creator God to lead us into new ways of creating. I felt this new painting was an improvement over the one that won first place. I got tired of staying in bed, but my illness allowed me to enjoy the artistic talent God had so graciously given me. My illness gave me the time to create a painting I still enjoy every day. I'm happy something good developed from that two month case of pneumonia. I had to stay on antibiotics all that time because of fever and a very slow recovery, which caused problems later producing an over abundance of the yeast, candida albicans.

Painting kept me content and occupied, so I no longer felt lonely, because my heavenly Father was there showing me how to apply every brush stroke on my painting.

I knew there was a reason for my suffering from so many infections and having to experience pain. Each thing that comes to me I know comes for a reason. Once I learned to trust God's reasoning rather than my own, I knew He allowed these things for my benefit even though I couldn't figure it out at the time. God could see the whole picture. Our lives are like a canvas God is painting. We need to understand that the difficult times are necessary to make the painting of our life vibrant and alive.

What brings light to our picture is knowing God's Son as our Savior and Lord. Jesus is Light and without Him our picture will be dark and hard to make out. We don't want a dull colorless painting to portray our life. Without the hard times the picture of our life might be just a cloudy blotch. Now when I suffer pain, I know God is working in me and I thank Him. Illness has become a benefit rather than a curse. With this new attitude I thank God for the hard times and the struggles. I know it is because He loves me. He's just adding some vivid color to the portrait of my life.

God, the Master Artist, works in and through me, giving me His time and His attention so that my life's portrait may be sharp and clear, full of life and beauty. He wants my portrait finished with a clear focus on His Son, my Lord Jesus.

My heavenly Father wants nothing to come between the relationship I have with my Lord and Savior, Jesus Christ.

When times are good be happy; but when times are bad, consider: God has made the one as well as the other (Ecclesiastes 7:14).

✿ Mother's Death—A Time of Reflection

While I was facing health problems I received a call from Daddy. "Your mama's gone," he told me. She'd died on the doctor's table while getting a treatment. The doctor had come out to the waiting room, called

Daddy into his office and told him, "Louise just died. I couldn't revive her; I did everything I knew how to do to bring her back."

Daddy was crying and broken with grief.

"Oh, Daddy, I'm so sorry. I know how much you loved Mom."

Daddy poured out how much she'd meant to him. "I just wish I'd been more loving to her," he reflected. "She never asked for much; I could have been more affectionate to her."

Later in our conversation I suggested maybe he ought to get an autopsy done.

"What good would that do? It wouldn't bring your mama back," Daddy answered.

I knew he was right. I told Daddy I wanted to remember my mom the way she was when I'd last seen her. I was in a state of shock. I felt pain, but I thanked God for the wonderful time He'd allowed Mother and me to have on my last visit.

My mother was dead and I knew she'd gone to be with our heavenly Father. I was thankful that my mother had such a strong faith in God and that she'd seen to it that I had been given good instruction in the Word. All I could remember was the mother I'd enjoyed so much during our last trip to Colorado. I knew I'd miss her, but my certainty of her being with her Lord and Savior was such a blessing, I wanted to praise God she belonged to Him and I could be assured of seeing her again one day.

Through the death of my mother I drew closer to my heavenly Father and I depended on Him to fulfill His promises.

Be faithful even to the point of death, and I will give you the crown of life (Revelations 2:10).

🏵 A Testing of Faith

My father had mourned my mother's passing for several years before he became very sick. At first he thought he had the flu and told me not to come back because I might get it. Later, he learned he had cancer of the stomach, and from lying in bed in the hospital and having poor circulation in his right leg, it turned black and pained him terribly.

He had loved taking ninety-mile bike trips to Glenwood Springs where he sat in the hot mineral caves, and finally swam in the largest outdoor mineral pool in the world. My dad really believed in exercise and keeping his body fit by eating healthy foods. Since Mother's death he'd gotten into the habit of drinking coffee and eating doughnuts. He felt sure that is what caused his stomach cancer. He and Mom had ridden a tandem bike to the airport every morning, but if they stopped for a drink it was milk or fruit juice, not coffee.

Until his trip to the hospital he'd still ridden to the airport every morning on his bicycle. He knew some of the regulars at the coffee shop and he could pour out his sorrow to them. While he talked he drank coffee and ate doughnuts. Dad's greatest pain was that Mom was no longer with him. Living without Mom was unbearable for him. They had really loved each other. The year Mom died would have been their fiftieth anniversary.

Finally, the doctors decided they had to amputate Dad's lower leg and foot. He went into a terrible depression. Since his leg wouldn't heal, I decided he must have diabetes like his sisters Anna and Alvina had. Anna had gone blind because of diabetes. I stayed in Colorado for awhile and tried to help my brother, Ronnie, with the housework and with spending time with our dad in the hospital. On my second trip back, my father's leg was still causing problems, because the last operation wouldn't heal.

One day my father would say, "I'll get an artificial leg and I'll ride my bike again." The next day he'd sit and cry and say how hopeless his life seemed. I saw where I got my mood swings. The higher my mood elevated one day, the lower it fell the next day.

When I decided to go home from my second trip, I went by the hospital to visit with my father for the last time. I held my father's hand and I looked deep into his eyes.

"You know, Daddy, if you believe what the Bible says about Jesus dying for your sins, when you die, God will take you to heaven and you'll be with Mom. After all, that is what you've wanted ever since Mother passed away. Death can be a happy time of rejoicing because you're going to be with mama in heaven." I kissed Daddy and left the hospital.

Not too many days later my brother called. "Dad died today," Ron told me. "What did you tell Dad? Gwennie, from the day you left he refused to eat again."

I told Ron what I'd told Dad. My brother, Henry, was especially thankful when years later I told him what I'd told Daddy and what his response had been. It assured Ronnie, Henry, and me that our father had faith in God and in life after death.

For to me, to live is Christ and to die is gain (Philippians 1:21).

7
Learning to Listen for God's Prompting

"My sheep listen to my voice; I know them, and they follow me" (John 10:27).

 The Day I Didn't Listen to God

 Following God's Inner Prompting

 Down to the Last Potato

Now choose life, so that you and your children may live and that you may love the Lord your God, listen to his voice, and hold fast to him (Deuteronomy 30:19b-20).

❀ The Day I Didn't Listen to God

"I don't need a physician," Mrs. Stephens told me the last time I visited her in the hospital. "The Lord is my Great Physician and He's the only one I'll ever need. I want to go be with Him and I want to be with my husband, Karl, too."

Although this wasn't yet in God's plan she did get her wish to leave the hospital and return home. I wondered how she'd ever get around with her feet swollen double their normal size. This little eighty-eight-year-old woman lived alone on several acres of ground, and at times she even chopped up wood that was too big for her little heating stove. Each evening after work her son checked on her to see if everything was okay.

On a warm summer day in Santa Cruz, California I was prompted to go visit her. Going to the hospital was easy, but I really didn't want to make the trip way out to that country road in Aptos. She was a delightful little German lady who belonged to our church. I really enjoyed my visits with her, but on that particular day I just didn't feel in the mood to go. It was too bad she didn't have a phone because then I could just call her. The urgency to call on her continued throughout the day, but I shrugged it off thinking, *I'll go another day when I feel more like going.*

I didn't get the chance to go another day.

Our pastor called to tell me that Mrs. Stephens had died. On that very day I'd been urged all day long to visit her, she'd fallen on the floor early in the morning while trying to put a large piece of wood in her heating stove to warm the house. That poor little lady lay where she'd fallen on her cold bare floor, from early in the morning until her son came by that night to check on her.

She'd twisted her leg so she couldn't get up. Her badly swollen feet were also a factor hindering her from getting on her feet. She'd even thrown something through the window to try and get attention from someone on the outside to come help her. She lived in a very damp and chilly place that never seemed to get any sunshine because of a large hill that blocked the sun. She became so chilled from lying on the floor she got pneumonia and died a few days later.

God had called me to go help that old woman and I wouldn't pay attention. I learned from that incident to listen for God's urging and to follow it. Often, we have only that moment to do or say what He wants, so I'll never again let the moments of His prompting pass unheeded. This was a hard way to learn a lesson, but after it happened, God certainly impressed on my mind the necessity to pay attention to Him.

I would have felt even more devastated if our pastor hadn't reminded me how badly Mrs. Stephens wanted to go be with her heavenly Father and join her husband, Karl. Time and again she'd told me she didn't need earthly physicians but that she wanted to meet the Great Physician beyond. She'd led a full life and she missed her dear departed husband, Karl. I knew that now she was where she'd wanted to be all along.

I also knew those urges to visit her were actually God's inner voice urging me to carry out His will. Now I know what people mean when they say "God's still small voice," and I decided to listen for His voice from that day on, following those urges that are in line with what the Bible teaches.

Do everything without complaining or arguing, so that you may become blameless and pure, children of God without fault in a crooked and depraved generation, in which you shine like stars in the universe (Philippians 2:14).

❀ Following God's Inner Prompting

How could a woman have lived eighty-nine years in this country and never heard the gospel message?

I was prompted to become a census taker in Santa Cruz county.

When I arrived at a home set off by itself and rang the door bell, I announced I was taking the census and asked, "How many people live at this residence?"

The little old woman standing in front of me started to cry. "I'm all alone here. My brother died last week."

"You aren't going to be alone any longer," I told her. God prompted me to tell her about Jesus—how when He came into your life you would never be alone again. From that day, I visited Mrs. Crandall at least twice a week, and I told her Jesus loved her and about how He died on the cross to save her from her sins. When I thought the time was right, I asked our pastor to visit her, too.

One day when I arrived she was all smiles. "Something happened that I think will make you happy," she told me.

"What is it?" I asked.

"The last time Pastor Carlsen visited me, I told him I trusted in Jesus to save me and I was baptized. Now I'm a member of God's family. When I die, He'll take me to heaven."

I hugged her. "You're right! That does make me happy because now you are my sister in Christ."

Mrs. Crandall wrote to tell her sister in New York about her new-found belief in Jesus and that she had been baptized. One day when I dropped by to visit, she handed me a letter from her sister to read. Her sister who was ninety-three, wrote that when she'd learned of her sister's salvation she had called a minister nearby and talked with him. He'd told her the same things her sister had written to her about Jesus. "I decided I wanted Jesus to save me from my sins, too. Now, we can be in heaven together," she wrote.

Wouldn't it have been sad had I not listened to my heavenly Father's prompting the day I stopped to take the census? Two lovely ladies might have died never knowing Jesus. Isn't it wonderful how God cares about each of us individually?

"I will be a Father to you and you, will be my sons and daughters," says the Lord Almighty (2 Corinthians 6:18).

*This article published as "Following God's Prompting" in the *Joyful Woman*, September/October, 1997. Also reprinted in *Beautiful Teen*, October, 1997. It appeared as "Following that Still Small Voice" in *The Wesleyan Woman*, Fall, 1997.

❀ Down to the Last Potato

One day I was taking a religious census, going door to door to see if there was anyone who was looking for a church to attend. I saw what looked just like a chicken coop. I wasn't going to stop there but that inner urging came again. I walked over and knocked on the door.

A woman came to the door, hunched over with her head sunk into drooping shoulders that were wrapped in a shawl to keep her warm. "Hello. I wasn't expecting anyone." She greeted me in a listless manner and invited me in. I stepped inside and sat on an orange crate. Sitting down I looked at what had once been an aristocratic face with high cheekbones, but now she appeared weathered and gaunt. Talking with this once lovely woman I learned that her name was Camille. At one time she and her husband had been quite wealthy but he'd had a heart attack. While he was unable to attend to his business, his partners had just written him out of the business.

These two people had never been in a spot like this before, where they needed help, and they had no idea where to go. I told Camille that we'd bring in hot meals and look for a warmer place for them to stay. Camille's husband was in his seventies, much older than she, who I guessed would probably be in her late forties or early fifties.

However, she'd suffered a nervous breakdown after her husband lost his business, and neither of them was capable of handling a job. They hadn't gone on welfare and they had no money—only one potato left in their pantry. Their place was not wired for gas or electricity and at this time of the year it was mighty chilly. Someone had let them live here until they could manage to afford a real house. I told her we'd do what we could for them, and we'd be over with hot food later that day.

When I got back home I called our pastor and he said he thought the church women could cook for them until they were able to care for themselves. I'd already planned a dinner to take them for that evening. Our pastor said he and his wife would fix them breakfast in the morning, and then we'd get a group of women lined up to fix meals. He asked if I could pick up and deliver the meals. I told him I would. He and I saw to it they had food in their place and we took them down to sign up for temporary aid, until they could get on their feet. Different people fixed hot meals and I delivered them.

I spoke with my doctor about this woman needing medical attention, and set her an appointment to see him. The pastor and I also found a more livable place for the couple, that had heat and lights. We helped them get signed up for assistance, and the owner let them move into the comfortable house we'd found for them to rent.

I can't think of anything more rewarding than helping people who really need help. These two people started to bloom. They joined our congregation and the following year he was elected president of the Board of Elders.

Suppose a brother or sister is without clothes and daily food. If one of you says to him; "Go, I wish you well; keep warm and well fed," but does nothing about his physical needs, what good is it? In the same way faith by itself, if it is not accompanied by action, is dead (James 2:15-17).

8

A New Church and New Problems

God was reconciling the world to himself in Christ, not counting men's sins against them. And he has committed to us the message of reconciliation (2 Corinthians 5:19).

 A New Congregation for Soquel

 A Difference of Opinions

 Becoming a Foster Mom

 A Disturbing Debate Provoked Questions

I appeal to you, brothers, in the name of our Lord Jesus Christ, that all of you agree with one another so that there may be no divisions among you and that you may be perfectly united in mind and thought (1 Corinthians 1:10).

❀ A New Congregation for Soquel

In May of 1958 my husband was transferred to the Santa Cruz area. For a number of months we attended Messiah Lutheran Church in Santa Cruz, which was quite a drive from where we'd purchased a home in Soquel, California. We learned a new congregation was needed for the areas surrounding Santa Cruz.

We combined with several other families to start a new congregation in Soquel. At first we had retired ministers preaching, but then we called Pastor Hermann and he accepted our call. Harold and I started a youth group. This was also a very rewarding group of kids to work with and we'd had plenty of practice in San Francisco.

I taught the teenage Sunday School Class as I had in San Francisco. No one enjoyed the league any more than I did. It was fun, educational, loving, caring, and nurturing for the kids I loved—teenagers. Our older daughter, Terry, was able to enjoy this league and it was a happy time for her as well.

After holding church services for more than a year in the IOOF Hall about two blocks from our house, we finally bought some ground, with the help of the Synod and a really fine church building was erected. It was high on a hill and they named it Mount Calvary. It was a lovely church where we could worship and hold our youth activities. Three crosses were strategically placed in front of the church to denote the three crosses visible when Jesus died.

Both of our daughters would end up being married in this delightful church building, which housed the congregation that Harold and I had been instrumental in establishing.

How lovely is your dwelling place, O Lord Almighty! (Psalm 84:1).

❀ A Difference of Opinions

What happened to change our happy existence?
Our Pastor Hermann, whom we all loved, was not yet fifty when a fatal heart attack struck him down in his prime. Although it was a terrible blow to our church, all the people joined together and kept the church going, with retired ministers filling in until we could call a new minister.

From the first night Harold met our new pastor things changed. Harold was the president of the board, and he and the newly called minister did not see eye to eye.

One thing that troubled Harold was this new minister's idea of having communion every Sunday. Harold felt that would make it seem commonplace and take away the special meaning of communion. I think both Harold and the new minister had valid reasons for the way they felt. Although it was a close vote, the congregation decided to accept the new pastor's wishes to administer communion each week.

Harold would sit with his arms folded across his chest and refuse to attend communion more than once a month. The expression on his face showed he was still angry because he'd been out-voted. I believe his anger opened the door for Satan to work in his life.

The new minister went back to Chicago and became involved with a group of ministers who were against the Vietnam War. Our pastor signed papers that he would work to discourage men from going to Vietnam, and the group he'd joined even encouraged draftees to burn their draft cards. Harold felt he was wrong. Harold told him, "If this is your opinion, that's okay, but it isn't the stand of the people in this congregation to burn draft cards or to actively work against the Vietnam War."

Everything was all right until a big article came out in the newspaper, telling of our pastor's stand and his being united with this anti-war group. The article was written as if our congregation backed his stand. Harold read the article and said, "That's it. We won't be going back to Mount Calvary." He forbade me to step foot in that church again.

We were two of the founders of that congregation and we'd been active for years. We had many dear friends we were leaving behind and I loved the teenage group there. It broke my heart that these two Christian men couldn't work out their disagreements. The pastor never even came to talk to us when we left. A number of other people left soon after and the church attendance dropped dramatically.

This was the beginning of the end of a wonderful life as I knew it.

Finally, all of you, live in harmony with one another; be sympathetic, love as brothers, be compassionate and humble (1 Peter 3:8).

Becoming a Foster Mom

I went to Juvenile Hall to interview fifteen-year-old Katie, a runaway, as a prospective foster child. At the time, it seemed that having another daughter Cindy's age would be a good idea. Cindy, at fourteen, thought it would be fun to have a sister. Katie appeared to be sweet and misunderstood. Shortly after she moved in, Cindy confided, "Mom, Katie is exactly the type of girl you wouldn't want me around and now she's my foster sister." I had led such a sheltered life I thought that no girl had sex before marriage.

The first time she ran off was with a wanted criminal who had an arsenal in his house. For hours I rode with the police trying to track down where this criminal was hanging out. The police wanted me to identify Katie. Even though back-up police were called to surround the house where the criminal had been staying and they surrounded the house with guns drawn, they found neither the criminal nor Katie.

That evening Katie called and asked if I would pick her up. All I thought about was, *Thank God Katie's safe.*

Being naive, I let Cindy and Katie double date. Little did I know that she talked Cindy into letting them drop her off so she and her boyfriend could go alone on their date.

About six months later, Cindy overheard Katie telling a couple of girls about the strict family she had to live with. Cindy came home furious. "She makes us sound like bad guys!" she fumed. Again I behaved with my head stuck in the sand, and made excuses for Katie. "Honey, she got off on the wrong foot and I would like to see her have a chance to be like other kids with a real family. Maybe you can be a good influence on her."

"I don't even like her," Cindy replied adamantly.

For the two years she was with us I had plenty of signals to tell me I was putting my daughter in harm's way, but when Katie attended confirmation class regularly for two years, I wanted her to learn God's will and follow it. I hoped because of those classes her soul would be saved eternally. If that was accomplished, then taking her in would be worth it. However, I couldn't save her from herself. She had a built-in pattern of being intimate with boys. I don't know if I was so blind at the time I didn't think about what Cindy might pick up by bringing Katie into our home, or if my hope and faith were so strong that we could help her, I didn't look at that side of the situation.

One thing really troubled me. Katie wet the bed, sometimes night after night. At first she took the sheets and hid them in a drawer and got clean ones and put them on her bed. But the room started smelling awful and I finally found the brown urine-stained sheets wadded up in a drawer. It meant doing loads of extra wash. This poor little fifteen-year-old girl who ran away to be with boys still wet the bed. I washed the linens and prayed for Katie.

Katie and Cindy were confirmed in pure white robes and we took pictures of the eventful day. I felt so happy knowing my girls had finished their confirmation and I don't think they missed any classes. Katie gave all the right answers to the questions Pastor Carlsen asked that day they were confirmed, so she had learned what the Bible said.

After three more times of taking off to find more boys that would fulfill what she felt she needed, I talked to her. "Katie, if you run away one more time, I'm not going to pick you up from Juvenile Hall," and I meant it. She wasn't getting better, she was pulling the same tricks she had with her mom, who they blamed for her problems. Well, I wasn't her real mom and she was still running away.

Our daughter wasn't doing well in school and I felt her reaction might be from Katie, since she'd always made high marks in the lower grades. Besides we weren't helping Katie. We were the wrong foster parents for her.

The phone rang one morning after Katie ran away again, and I said, "I'm sorry, but I'm not helping Katie. I'm just letting her carry on the same way she did with her mom. Keep her at Juvenile Hall and maybe another foster mother will have more influence on her than I've had." I had even sewed dresses for her that just fit beautifully.

I don't like to fail at the things I do, and I truly felt like a 100 percent failure when it came to Katie. The woman that placed her with us heard the sorrow in my voice and now she was concerned about me. I did feel really broken up that I'd failed so miserably with Katie. Me, the counselor for scads of teens and I couldn't even help this one girl. I had no desire to try another foster child. I'd had it!

I heard from Katie once after that. She came to our house with a policeman boyfriend. He was such a proper-seeming young man. He was cute, intelligent and seemed to honestly care about Katie. I was pleased to see a policeman at her side instead of chasing her.

Last Sunday I talked to my daughter Cindy about Katie. Cindy surprised me when she said that she remembers her time with Katie with fond memories.

"I didn't like the things she did, but I really grew to love her," she said. "I think wherever Katie is she probably thinks about those times with us as one of the good times of her life. I think she did learn a lot while she lived with us. At least our hearts were in the right place when we tried our best to help her. I'll bet she remembers when we used to mimic Lily Tomlin."

Cindy recalled when she and Katie laughed so hard while doing imitations of Lily Tomlin, tears rolled out of their eyes, and down their cheeks.

Maybe our having a foster daughter wasn't quite the failure I thought it was.

How happy I was to hear my daughter's feelings about Katie after all these years.

For if the willingness is there, the gift is acceptable according to what one has, not according to what he does not have (2 Corinthians 8:12).

🌼 A Disturbing Debate Provoked Questions

We had driven a few miles further and attended Christ Lutheran Church in Aptos, and we soon became Youth Counselors there. Harold became very involved with the working of the congregation and became the superintendent of the Sunday School. One week, when our pastor was gone, Harold preached the sermon and I wept because it was so touching. Visitors said, "That man has to be a pastor. No one preaches like that without training."

The pastor had gone back to attend the Bethel Series and came home all fired up to get it in the church. Harold worked overtime and gave the first large sum of money to get the series started. I attended the teachers' class of the Bethel Series taught by Pastor Carlsen. Some of the teachers taught the members of the congregation.

After we had attended this church for maybe five years, Pastor Carlsen asked Harold if he would play Satan in a program where he, as our pastor, would be talking for God and the teachings of the church. Harold would represent Satan and try to show that Christ wasn't really necessary. Harold studied and studied his part and he paced back and forth questioning the pastor at every turn. He'd learned his part by memory and the pastor was reading much of his part.

From what I witnessed, Satan clearly won the debate. What the pastor said indicated the way Christians believe is right. Harold's argument was Satan's lies. The little skit disturbed me. Harold's portrayal and the way he emphasized his words was the same way Satan convinces people that what he's telling them is true. Of course the skit was not written for Satan to win the debate, but Harold was far more convincing than our pastor was.

The pastor announced from the pulpit: "Mr. Walden was just playing the part of Satan, but that is not what he himself believes." Harold played his role so convincingly many of the children from Sunday School had questioned the pastor asking if that was what Mr. Walden really believed.

I look back now and wonder if Satan wasn't already playing a part in Harold's life. This took place shortly before we had to leave and move to San Jose.

We must have attended this church about seven years before Harold was transferred to San Jose. We'd both worked hard in many areas of the church and we were given another surprise party, this time by the members of the congregation.

The party had been held at Joanne and Don Wilden's lovely big home. They'd invited us for dinner and we had no idea most of the congregation would be there. When we walked in we heard, "Surprise!" The place was packed with people who loved us and appreciated our work in the church. They had brought us a money gift to use in our new home. The food had been furnished by the members and it was a lovely party. We had loved this congregation of people and we were sad to be leaving, but I didn't have any idea that our lives would soon change drastically.

I certainly never foresaw the future, but God knew all about what would happen in San Jose.

"See to it then, that the light within you is not darkness" (Luke 11:35).

9

My
Wilderness Years

*I am in pain and distress; may your salvation,
O God, protect me…. You are my help and my
deliverer; O Lord, do not delay* (Psalm 69:27,70:5b).

🌸 My Wilderness Years

🌸 Our Thirty Year Wedding Anniversary

🌸 Our Marriage Takes a Downward Spiral

🌸 Gaining Perspective from a "Perfect" Marriage

*Remember how the Lord your God led you all the way
in the desert these forty years, to humble you and to
test you in order to know what was in your heart,
whether or not you would keep his commands*
(Deuteronomy 8:2).

❀ My Wilderness Years

My wilderness years were times of darkness, discouragement, confusion, and depression with the devil taunting me on the sidelines. These were times in my life when it seemed God couldn't hear my prayers, and there were days when I felt He had forgotten all about me. My first journey into bleak areas came in my late twenties when I experienced four operations in five years and even more operations followed.

One surgery followed another. It was good to get the pain out of my right wrist by having a ganglion removed, because even writing hurt my wrist. It was a blessing to finally find a doctor who knew what it was and how to remove it.

Then a mole on my right thigh didn't look right. Doctors gave me something to put on it, but in two weeks a small mole had grown as large as a fifty cent piece and surgery was performed at once. They took the mole out just as it was turning into melanoma. It made the cover of a Physicians magazine.

My back gave me problems from the time I was hit riding my bike. My regular doctor felt it was time for me to see a neurosurgeon and his decision was to operate. I recovered remarkably fast and in five days they said I could go home and do whatever I wanted, with the exception of heavy lifting or moving a piano. I took the doctor at his word and started doing exactly as I had before surgery.

Everything was going smoothly. After three months I was in our basement taking laundry out of the dryer and my back convulsed in a profusion of spasms doubling me over. I couldn't straighten up. I managed to crawl up my stairs and get in bed. I couldn't move without more spasms seizing my muscles.

Over a period of several years I returned four times to the hospital where therapists reported the spasms were the type polio victims have. The therapist would put hot compresses on my back and work to get one spasm stopped and others would convulse right above or below the original spasm. They would just keep moving all up and down my body. Later I learned I have scoliosis, and that can produce muscle spasms. It seemed strange no doctor told me. Now I wonder if having the ruptured disc removed, may have severely affected my already curved spine.

During the years of spasms the orthopedic physician and the neurosurgeon both decided I could be put in a body cast to try and stop the spasms.

I thought it would weaken my muscles to be in a cast for six months or longer and I didn't go for it.

Now I realize that might have helped my curved spine.

I couldn't stand or walk because of spasms. When I tried to get on my feet I remained bent over. We had a woman from church who came in to cook and watch the children. I read the Bible a great deal lying in bed and I had more time to think and pray.

I finally prayed the prayer of relinquishment, telling the Lord that if it was His will for me to remain unable to walk, I would accept that fact. God approves when we put things into His hands. After that I started getting better but another problem surfaced that had been troubling me for years. My gynecologist felt that I had several female problems that might be contributing to some intense pain I'd endured since a teenager, and he felt even the spasms might be intensified by an internal problem. He hadn't wanted to perform a hysterectomy because of my age. However, he scheduled me for surgery and once they opened me up they found that I had been bleeding internally for some time. Endometriosis had spread to my stomach walls and even my appendix which was also removed. I had Endometriosis on my ovaries as well, but they managed to leave a small portion of my left ovary, to try and prevent sudden shock from a hysterectomy at my young age of thirty. They left me completely sedated for three days because the surgery was so extensive. However that surgery did a great deal to relieve much of the pain I had been suffering. It was then I started back working with the youth league as their counselor and taught the teenage Bible Class at Grace Lutheran Church in San Francisco.

I no longer questioned what God was doing while I was serving the youth. My time in bed strengthened my faith and made me a more vibrant and faith-filled counselor.

My toughest wilderness experience started soon after Harold was transferred to San Jose and I had to leave behind the elderly people I visited including Ms. Crandall to whom I had grown very attached. She's the one I met taking the census. All my very close friends were in the Santa Cruz area. Thankfully, one close couple, Ann and Frank Phillips, lived in Novato, north of San Francisco and we saw them about every other month.

Soon after our daughter Cindy was married, I came down with pneumonia which lasted a long two months. The prolonged course of antibiotics which I took, contributed to a Candida-related disease which caused an abnormal growth of yeast in my digestive tract, which in turn brought about problems with digesting certain foods. Migraines started around the same time. The horrible morning headaches I awakened with came as a result of my eating the foods I had grown extremely allergic to. One-sided headaches—diagnosed migraines—caused visual disturbances and nausea before they started.

Both my mother and her father, had suffered with these headaches. Since mine were mainly caused by oats, corn, and wheat, the pills for migraines weren't working very well because I kept eating granola with wheat and oats, the very foods causing the headaches. It is similar to someone who drinks coffee and quits. Because their system craves more coffee they get a headache, and drinking coffee will relieve the headache. The cereal also relieved my headache temporarily, but it always returned.

These horrible headaches with vision problems and nausea continued over seventeen years, quite steadily. Sometimes one headache lasted for two weeks. Actually, they have never stopped completely, but now I know how to get them stopped.

I started complaining and whining about my lot in life, just as the Israelites did after God delivered them out of Egypt. While I taught Sunday School, I'd been hard on the Israelites for their lack of gratitude and their disrespect toward God, after He provided them daily with manna when they wandered in the wilderness for forty years; and yet I became caught up in some of their same sins of grumbling and complaining. I focused on the bad incidents in my life instead of praising God for the blessings He gave me. I was focusing on the way I felt and my emotions and I wanted God to answer my prayers in my way, instead of trusting that He knew what was best for me. I was a sorry excuse for a Christian.

I faced many changes. Empty nest syndrome, deprivation of hormones, and extreme allergies. It was a heavy load and I'm sure I wasn't the best company. I tried to get out and help people in nursing homes and I ended up feeling I ought to be in there with them. Besides, they wanted me to call bingo numbers, and I wanted to relate to the people personally as I had in Santa Cruz. I was extremely depressed. My housekeeping grew terrible. I slept most of the time.

Harold would tell me before he left in the morning: "Don't worry about getting up; just stay in bed. There's nothing you have to do."

I felt useless, worthless and terribly sad.

When he came home in the evening I wanted him to hold me and love me, but he brought home files to work on or reports to write. Making love or holding me was the last thing he had on his mind.

The way was left open for Satan to whisper his lies into my subconscious, bringing me into a state of despair and negativity. I honestly don't understand why we humans fall for his lies. Listening to him we grow deeper and deeper into despair. I really needed something to fight the depression I didn't realize I had until much later.

I never became involved with liquor or drugs, only pills to try and stop the headaches which sometimes didn't stop for two weeks. I was worn out from pain. Meanwhile Satan taunted me with thoughts of hopelessness and defeat.

While I was just getting over my long siege with pneumonia and still felt weak, my father had called to tell me my mother passed away. I had enjoyed such a wonderful time with her on my last trip right before she died, that I wanted to remember her that way and I didn't attend the funeral. Harold wouldn't take off time to go with me and I wasn't physically strong enough to go alone. By not attending the funeral, I was not putting a closure on Mother's death. With her death I once again recalled the hurtful way she'd treated me. I couldn't seem to let go of reliving my hurtful days at home. I'd started going over each hurtful thing Mother had said to me, playing those records over in my mind, day after day. However, when I thought about the good times we had the last time we were together it helped tremendously.

I honestly didn't understand I was holding unforgiveness toward her in my heart. I'd been remembering those things she told me since I was quite small, and it had become a habit for me to go over and over them in my head. I had become a victim of my past.

The devil is no gentleman. He hits us where we hurt and when we're down. He didn't want me to forget my painful past or forgive my mother. A few years later my dad died. Now, I had no parents to turn to.

Only God's being with me could have gotten me through those years.

God allowed me to face the furnace of affliction and Satan's trying to encroach upon my spirit, weighing me down with guilt, self-pity, and unforgiveness.

We had moved close to a gym where I was a member, and that was one time I got out and talked with other people while working to keep my body in shape. At this time I met Julie, whom I speak of in chapter fourteen. She remembers my pain.

That story proves I hadn't lost my faith, because I was witnessing even during the wilderness years. I knew my great need for my Lord Jesus, and I prayed, but those prayers lacked the faith they needed to be answered, or it just wasn't time for God to act.

I had started selling cosmetics at home parties, so I still had some contact with people. Harold drove me to the place where the party was held and came and picked me up. Harold wrote the checks; I guess he bought the food. The days passed and I was so depressed, but I had no idea that it was depression I was feeling, along with grief and a lack of hormones. I was just going through the motions of living. I had no idea of what real life was, until years later.

I really never grieved for my parents so I stayed in a constant state of heartache, carrying a heavy burden, feeling oppressed, and at times hopeless; but I still knew moments of joy despite sinus, ear, bladder, and kidney infections, which never ended.

I saw to it that I got to church on Sunday, and I loved worshipping God. But going from church to church, I never got to put roots down or get into any programs. Good sermons could have done more to help. They give you something to think about all week.

God's Spirit was with me. He didn't leave me alone. He slowly taught me to focus my quiet moments on Him. I finally found that praising God and thanking Him, rather than complaining about my lot in life, made me much happier. That realization didn't come easy.

What I am confessing here is true of many people who just don't realize why their lives are so bleak and unrewarding. People try to live in their own strength and it is miserable. We need Jesus' power and strength to live abundant lives. Then we also receive His joy and His wisdom. We begin seeing things through His eyes, and life becomes exciting—the way God intended man and woman to be when He created Adam and Eve, before they disobeyed Him.

Later, I would learn that obedience to God brings joy!

My life remained difficult until I recognized my inadequacy in dealing with life on my own. I needed to surrender and allow God to take over, but the time was not quite right. God was allowing me to do things my way until I learned my way didn't work.

Making the decision to place my full weight on Jesus' strength and power was not easy. It's a hard decision to make because I felt I'd lose my own identity. But at this time, most of my identity had been given over to Harold. Very little of me was left.

I'd lost the artistic, energetic, positive person who I once was. And even when I had my own identity, I had nothing of worth to offer my Lord, because the Bible says, *All have sinned and fall short of the glory of God* (Romans 3:23).

Jesus was God in human form. He didn't fall short of the glory of God because He was without sin. He overcame the temptation of the devil, our flesh, and the world. Unlike the first Adam, Jesus pleased God.

Because Jesus is perfect He wanted to give me an abundant life in Him.

It took some time before I quit wandering in the wilderness and came into the Light of God's love. His love was there. It was available, but I still had to understand the necessity of placing my full weight on Jesus' power and strength.

A sister in Christ who has gone through the process of finding Jesus for her life told me: "Now I know what life is supposed to be, and I never want to get caught up in those bad things I used to do. That wasn't life. That was miserable. Only Jesus gives us life!"

Stop wandering in the wilderness and come into the Light of God's love.

And he died for all, that those who live should no longer live for them-selves but for him who died for them and was raised again (2 Corinthians 5:15).

❀ Our Thirty Year Wedding Anniversary

Our thirty year wedding celebration wasn't fun like our twenty-fifth had been. We celebrated by going out to dinner with one of our favorite couples, Hank and Coreen Dyrdahl. Harold's and my conversations seemed forced instead of spontaneous and full of fun. I was glad my good friend, Coreen, agreed to celebrate with us, because she was full of life and delight-ful to be around. The evening was pleasant and it was good to know we'd made it thirty years, even though I was quite aware that our marriage was-n't all that it should be.

Later Coreen said, "On your anniversary, you and Harold sure weren't the same couple I once knew."

Now I needed to find a close friend like Coreen in San Jose. I put my foot down and picked the church I'd liked the best, and told Harold I wanted to join so I could get to know some women there. I made the mistake of picking a church at least eight miles from our house, so I really needed a ride to get there. We attended church on Sundays, but I didn't get involved with the things during the week. I needed a good Bible Study and Christian friends to talk to. My close friends all seemed so far away. I slept much of the time, because I couldn't face the truth that our once wonderful marriage was in shambles.

What really disturbed me was that Harold wasn't even saying the Lord's Prayer in church. *How could a man who had worked so hard to spread God's Word now refuse to even pray in church?* It wasn't easy for me to talk to Harold and tell him how I felt, because he'd just dismiss whatever I said as "hogwash."

I talked to Jesus when I couldn't talk to anyone else, but I didn't feel Him directing me in any certain way. Days seemed so long and I felt so lonely. Mom and Dad were dead. Terry was so far away in Virginia, and Cindy was just starting out in her marriage and I didn't want to bring my grief to her.

I tried to understand what had changed Harold's faith. His being so angry when he didn't get his way about communion being only once a month, and then refusing to attend communion more often than once a month might have been the beginning of his loss of faith. He looked very angry when he sat with his arms folded across his chest, refusing the Lord's Supper. I think Satan used his anger to make inroads into his faith, and little by little the evil one whittled away his belief in God, until he questioned the Word the same way he had in the beginning.

But that didn't explain how he could have given that wonderful sermon at Christ Lutheran when Pastor was back east training for the Bethel Series.

Then, I recalled that Harold had been irate when Cindy moved in with her boyfriend before their marriage. He kept saying it hadn't done any good to raise her up in the church and he was very upset about that; and Cindy did get married just about the time we came to San Jose, to please her father. People may let us down, but God is faithful.

Be self-controlled and alert. Your enemy the devil prowls around like a roaring lion looking for someone to devour (1 Peter 5:8).

Our Marriage Takes a Downward Spiral

One day I was painting a watercolor and Harold stopped to take a look. "I don't see why you bother with that. You're really not very good at it," he observed. My painting slowed dramatically after that. My art teacher at school had admired my painting skills; and I had won first place in an art contest in Santa Cruz, but his unkind words cut into a hobby I had loved. Harold found fault with my friends, and even with the way I walked. "You walk just like Groucho Marks," he chided.

I'd had a critical mother and now a critical husband and at times I was even harder on myself than they were. I'm sure much of my low self-esteem came from all three sources, and I was feeling particularly depressed because of my parents' deaths coming so very close together.

I was unaware of the hidden disease which had been battering away at me for many years. I would awaken around three in the morning with an unbearable pain in the left side of my head and face. I found if I would get up and eat several bowls of the luscious granola type cereal, the headache would be better when I would awaken the second time in the morning. Then I would eat another bowl or two of the tempting cereal, and later in the day I'd eat it for a snack. I knew nothing of addictive reactions to foods, so before I went to bed I'd eat another bowl of the granola cereal. I was finishing off two large boxes of cereal each week. Several handfuls of the cereal during the day would tone down the terrible headaches. Oats, wheat, honey, brown sugar, nuts, dates, or maybe raisins were all good healthy foods. I added milk and sometimes a banana.

I was completely unaware that I had built an addictive allergy to the wheat and oats in this cereal. Wheat gives me terrible migraine headaches and oats still has a tendency to turn me into an argumentative one-way person.

Even after staying off of oats for many years and trying it again, having oatmeal for breakfast and two oat bars in the morning and two more at night, I once again became unreasonable with my older daughter who I had never had problems being around. It shocked even me. After my daughter was kind enough to help me after a foot operation, I told her to leave my house after eating the oatmeal and oatmeal bars.

I found myself doubting this whole allergy thing, and then another episode causes the same reaction and I realize once again, that particular food is not supposed to be in my diet. Some things are permanently difficult to eat and some are okay after you take a rest from having them in your diet. Apples were able to be reintroduced into my diet after a wait of several years. A friend of mine told me her allergic friend, who could not eat apples, had tried Fugi apples and they worked okay. I'm happy to say I can handle cooked Fugi apples every couple of weeks now. Often a food can be eaten again after leaving it out of the diet for six months. But on the second try the reaction to the food may flare up and respond the same way it once did. Then I wait a year or two, but often the food still bothers me and I know I must leave it alone.

There are many things other than foods that also bother me. Formaldehyde used on things as a disinfectant, or a preservative to make things last, affects me terribly.

The smell of jasmine plants in our backyard makes me agitated. Smelling odors like jasmine can raise my blood pressure. Getting away from constant irritating smells by taking a vacation helps because I'm away from the same types of trees and shrubs.

I feel wonderful on cruises, because we spend much of the time on water away from the blooming trees and shrubs. In ports they have different flora than we do at home

The constant smell of cigarette smoke for many years which still bothers me, caused my face to feel as if someone was holding a match an inch from my skin. The burning sensation was also a continual source of irritation during the years Harold smoked in the house. I had constant ear and sinus infections, my doctor felt were intensified by Harold's smoking. "I can't believe your husband would rather keep you on antibiotics than to quit smoking," my ear specialist told me.

These factors, combined with my push for more freedom, caused Harold to comment, "I don't like the way you are now. I want the old Gwen back."

The old Gwen loved and adored Harold. The old Gwen would laugh when he would get mad and tease him out of it. When he forbade the old Gwen to work or to drive a car, the "old Gwen" accepted it. The "new Gwen" challenged him when he spoke of his hatred for certain people. She no longer accepted his continual smoking and blowing smoke in her face, and she complained about the burning sensation she felt when he smoked around her.

Smoke hadn't hurt like that early in the marriage, but as the allergy grew, the pain grew more intense. Harold was retaliating to a person who was reacting to most foods, and from environmental stresses such as gas fumes, perfumes, and fertilizers. I was physically, mentally, and emotionally affected, but I didn't know it yet.

When I recalled the years of feeling so miserable, I became aware how this illness grew and grew until my actions and reactions were so affected, that I began to believe that this person was really me. I had been a positive person who became negative. My not being involved in Bible studies and teaching Sunday School had cut down on my reading the Word, and it was easier for me to slip into a more self-centered mode. By not putting our roots down in a church, I did not get involved by helping others. My life has always been more joyful when I am working with others to bring them closer to their Lord.

The doctor who had nursed me through two rough months of pneumonia recognized I had a problem, and he talked to me like a grandfather. He pushed his thumb against the desk, as if squashing a bug. "Someone has been holding you under their thumb all your life," he told me.

I didn't quite understand what he meant.

"I'd like to talk to you and your husband together."

I told my doctor I'd ask Harold about it.

I knew Harold kept me from doing things by telling me I wasn't mechanically inclined and that I was too clumsy. He wanted to keep me from working because he felt I should stay home with our girls, but now our daughters were grown and married.

I got a job in Soquel working at the pharmacy, and walked back and forth to work. I had also worked from age fourteen until seventeen when I married Harold. I needed to feel I was doing something worthwhile.

Then I recalled something the psychologist had said to me after she'd worked with our daughter, Cindy, one day. "Cindy will be all right. She's old enough that she'll be leaving and making a home of her own, soon. It's you I'm worried about. You're a lovely woman and I hate to see you staying where you are."

I didn't understand exactly what she meant, or perhaps I didn't want to know. After all, I thought that once married, you stayed married. I knew she must have seen something that concerned her during her discussion with Harold and me, when we talked to her about the troubles our daughter, Cindy, was having.

Harold finally said he would meet with my current doctor and I set up an appointment for him to talk with us together. In a roundabout way, by giving examples, Dr. Dickerson showed that people needed freedom to be themselves. He did it in such a conversational way, he didn't sound as if he was trying to find fault with anyone.

However, Harold heard it differently. "I can't wait until Dr. Dickerson dies," he told me later. "It can't be soon enough for me and I don't want to see or talk with him again." Dr. Dickerson had cancer and was quite ill, but he'd taken his time to try and help us.

Our new pastor in the church we finally decided to join, was having a class for couples on the subject of making marriages better. I begged and finally Harold went.

The pastor passed out paper and pencils and asked each of us to list five things we liked about our mate. I started writing but Harold refused to write anything.

"There must be something you like about Gwen. After all, you married her," our pastor chided.

Harold ignored the pastor and looked at me. "I'm leaving. If you want a ride home you'd better go with me, or you can take the bus home."

I was so crushed that he couldn't think of one good thing to write about me that I left with him. Besides I had no money for the bus.

After church one Sunday we'd stopped to buy a couple of items. I was standing by the cash register smiling because I always loved to worship and praise God. Suddenly Harold knocked into me stepping right on my foot. "Why are you standing there smiling like a Cheshire cat?"

I decided not to spoil my good mood by getting into a squabble. "I'm smiling because I was thinking about how happy I am after worshipping God."

I knew our marriage was in trouble but I didn't know what to do. I read first, second, and third John over and over. One passage told me, *If anyone says, "I love God," yet hates his brother he is a liar. For anyone who does not love his brother, whom he has seen, cannot love God, whom he has not seen.* Harold spoke often about hating people, and that didn't fit the Bible's description of a follower of Jesus.

Day after day he challenged my faith and he kept asking the question, "Why do you still believe? You know it doesn't work."

The only thing Harold hadn't been able to manipulate in my life was my belief in God, which was too important for me to give up. I told him I hated his constant questioning me about why I still believed in God. This angered him, and finally caused him to tip his hand and to speak of Jesus in an irreverent way, making a blasphemous statement about the One I loved more than him.

"You can say what you will about me, but I will not allow you to blaspheme the name of my Lord!" I told Harold.

If Harold had never known the glory of God I might have been able to think he spoke out of ignorance. But he had known Jesus and had spoken of his love for Jesus and ministered to others, and then to curse Jesus, showed me he no longer cared about my love for God or for him. According to the Bible, once a man believes and turns away from his faith his condition is worse than in the beginning.

Harold had taught teenagers the wonder of what Christ had done and then he returned to his original unbelief. (2 Peter 2:20-22 describes such people.)

I couldn't live with Harold under these conditions, because my faith in God and in Jesus Christ as my Savior and Lord, was more important than a thirty-two year relationship, no matter how good and comfortable it was or how deplorable it had been.

I told Harold I wanted a separation. He complied by saying, "You might make it alone for about a week, but you'll never be able to live on your own. In two weeks you'll be begging me to come back."

Harold didn't have any idea what I could do or become by placing my dependence upon God's strength, rather than relying on him.

Therefore I tell you that no one who is speaking by the Spirit of God says, "Jesus be cursed," and no one can say, "Jesus is Lord," except by the Holy Spirit (1 Corinthians 12:3).

❁ Gaining Perspective from a "Perfect" Marriage

I woke up one morning and wanted to find where I'd gone wrong.

One of the smartest things I did after filing for divorce, was to get into a class of women who were trying to find out what had gone wrong with their marriages. It was held at a Catholic church, and the therapist was Ann, a lovely Christian psychologist.

We would sit in two chairs. Our therapist, Ann, would assume the role of our husband and we would react the way we reacted to our husband. If Ann didn't sound like our husband we explained a little more about our husband's role.

What I found out was that I had married so young, I'd simply allowed Harold to take over where my father left off. He'd told me what I could and couldn't do and I obeyed him. As long as I did what he said we got along fine. When I tried to break out of the father-child relationship, Harold felt threatened. He was threatened when I wanted to drive, work, or exert my independence in any manner. When I wanted to do something other than what he suggested, he would manipulate my thinking until I cried to do what he'd wanted all along.

I also sat in his chair so I could learn where he had been coming from. We started off in a parent-child relationship and since I was happy to allow that relationship, it worked. When I tried to break out and become an adult, Harold immediately tried to keep me under his thumb so I couldn't leave him the way his mother had left him when he was three.

His great uncle raised him on a farm in Missouri. Harold realized that his Aunt was not his real mother but Uncle Charlie became his dad. His dad died of pneumonia when he was quite young so Harold didn't remember him. His mother rarely visited. She kept his sister Helen with her, but she had to earn a living and thought Harold would be better off on his great uncle's farm. His great uncle and his wife had been unable to have children, so Harold's mother took him there and dropped him off, much like people drop off stray kittens or dogs, hoping someone else will be happy to take them in.

His uncle was a hard man who worked Harold like a ranch hand. He was up early doing chores before school and back to work when he arrived home, and did his homework whenever he could fit it in. According to him, he often got his homework in one class for the next one coming up.

I could feel the hostility he harbored toward his great Uncle Charlie. I asked him many times if we could go back and see his "dad" but he was against it. I told him he needed to forgive his dad and make amends. He had left home at fifteen and never returned. I finally convinced him to make the trip when our Terry was thirteen and Cindy eight.

Harold's step-aunt had died some years before, and Charlie married Vivian. They met us at the airport and I hit it off great with both of them. Harold was a little stiff around them. When we arrived at the house, we found a very comfortable place except for the bathroom floor which had rotted through.

Harold bought some lumber, sawed out the rotted material, and fixed up the under flooring and laid in particle board. Together we bought new linoleum that matched what was in the bathroom, and Harold fixed up the floor as good as new.

Vivian was a good cook and we had some elegant meals. The big meal, dinner, was between noon and one o'clock. Vivian fed us like farm hands who needed a large noon meal to build enough energy to go out and plow and plant and work the farm.

When Harold called Charlie, "Dad," the first time, I nearly cried. By the time we left their Missouri home, these two men were once again father and son. I was happy I had played a part in reuniting this old and very deaf father and the son he'd raised until he was fifteen. Harold quit school and took off to work in another state, but finally came back, finished his schooling, and graduated as valedictorian of his class.

Although he lived somewhere in town he never visited the mom and dad who had raised him until our trip back with his daughters.

It was a trip of reunion for Harold and his dad, a trip of meeting the family for Terry, Cindy, Vivian, and me. It was a time of unspoken forgiveness and helpfulness for Harold, and it was a worthwhile journey that I'm glad we made.

One day I finally understood why Harold couldn't allow me to become an adult. When I'd asked for a separation, he'd said, "I always knew you'd leave me." I had never given him a reason to believe that was true. He was so sure I'd reject him he couldn't take the chance of letting me grow up. Yet, he felt so certain he would be rejected, he treated me in such a way that he made certain his prediction came true.

From this marriage I had learned never to allow a husband to become a father to me. From one of Harold's last statements, I learned it wasn't wise to marry someone and then expect them to change. When Harold and I split up he gave me good advice. "Whatever you do don't try to change your next husband." He made me painfully aware that I had contributed to the breakup of my marriage and that I had some changing to do myself.

Here is a trustworthy saying: If we died with him, we will also live with him; if we endure, we will also reign with him. If we disown him, he will disown us; if we are faithless, he will remain faithful, for he cannot disown himself (2 Timothy 2:11-13).

10

Love: His Banner Over Me

... Husbands ought to love their wives as their own bodies. He who loves his wife loves himself. After all, no one ever hated his own body, but he feeds and cares for it, just as Christ does the Church (Ephesians 5:28).

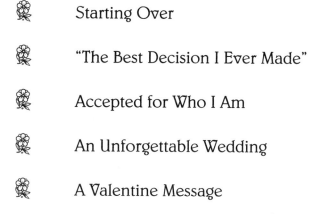

Starting Over

"The Best Decision I Ever Made"

Accepted for Who I Am

An Unforgettable Wedding

A Valentine Message

My Rest in the Storms of Life

Be imitators of God, therefore, as dearly loved children and live a life of love, just as Christ loved us and gave himself up for us as a fragrant offering and sacrifice to God (Ephesians 5:1-2).

❀ Starting Over

It was 1978, and I had taken a friend's advice not to sit around and mope. I'd come to an orientation meeting of Parents Without Partners in San Jose. Across from me sat the most handsome man I'd ever seen. *He'll never notice me with that beautiful blonde sitting beside him,* I thought. But when the break came he asked, "Would you like a cup of coffee?"

I hate coffee, but I wasn't about to say, "No," and ruin my chance to talk with this good looking man. "Why yes, that would be nice," I answered. I couldn't help but notice his striking profile when he was getting the coffee. When he walked back toward me and handed me the cup of coffee I felt an exciting jolt I'd never felt before. There wasn't one thing about this man that didn't appeal to me. His mustache was just a pleasant decoration on his upper lip and his eyes twinkled when he smiled. I don't remember anything about what we said during the break; I was so busy remembering everything about him, the way he walked and his wonderful voice when he talked. I later learned he'd played many leads in plays back in the St. Paul-Minneapolis area. At the conclusion of the meeting he walked me to my car. I was delighted he wanted to see me to my car, but I was also ashamed because I'd had a number of accidents while going through my divorce, and though the dents had been pounded out, they had just been given an undercoat of paint. I should have been thankful the dents were no longer visible.

Kerry handed me his card and I learned he was a Casualty Claim Manager for an insurance company and that his real name was Kerron. When I asked him about the spelling of his name he told me it had been his grandfather's name and had originated with his Irish ancestors. He told me I could just call him, Kerry.

When we got to my car I felt embarrassed for him to see that both my front and back fenders were painted and a side door and the trunk also had an undercoat of paint too. He didn't seem to hold that against me. His acceptance of me gave me a new feeling of self-worth.

"Are you planning to go to the dance Friday night?" he asked.

I hadn't thought about it until that moment and I'd never danced in my life, but if there was the chance to see Kerry again, I'd go. "Yes, I'll probably be there," I answered, not wanting to sound too anxious.

"I'll try to make it too, and I'll look for you," he told me.

From the time I arrived at the dance, men had asked me to dance and

I truthfully told them I'd never danced before, but that didn't seem to keep them from wanting to dance with me. Since I was always out on the dance floor I didn't see Kerry when he arrived.

When the band took their half-time break, I walked around the big dance floor and looked to see if I could find Kerry. We almost ran into each other while we were both hunting for one another.

Seeing him again gave me that same thrill I'd felt the night I'd met him. Dancing with Kerry was wonderful. When there was a dance where we danced apart from each other, Kerry had a fancy set of footwork that really looked like he knew what he was doing. When I told him I'd always wanted to take dance lessons and I'd gotten a notice from the park department that they were starting a dance class, he seemed excited. "Let's go together and take dance lessons," he suggested. I took no time at all to tell him I thought that was a wonderful idea. Later when he kissed me goodnight, I'd never felt the way I did when his arms were around me, and I'd never had such a reaction to a kiss before. I would say that I was captivated by Kerry right from the beginning. I think he was attracted to me but it took him longer to decide that I was the one for him.

Kerry told me that he'd have to miss at least one dance class because he'd promised his daughters that he would spend the Christmas and New Years' holidays with their three families. With Kerry leaving, I decided to go out with a man who'd been asking me for a date. He drove us over to Monterey for the day. It's a lovely drive and Monterey is a beautiful place. We had a late lunch on the wharf. What a beautiful view. We had good conversation, but by the time he drove me home I knew I'd seen enough of Charlie to last me a lifetime.

I dated several fellows and most of them just made Kerry seem better than ever. A math professor seemed to like my company and I liked his, because he had a jolly disposition. He was a Christian and he was an interesting conversationalist. He just wanted a woman to go places with him. He didn't seem to want any serious relationship with anyone.

I just wished Kerry would become a Christian and speak about his faith the way Albert did. When we went on outings with our church singles' group, Albert always took the seat beside me, and I found him to be an extremely interesting person to talk to and I admired his faith in God.

I started praying that Kerry would come to know Jesus.

Kerry stayed on his trip until after New Years and it seemed like an eternity. The night he called after arriving back home, I was so happy to hear his voice. He'd missed me, too, but he'd been busy with his daughters' families.

The night he came back from his visit to southern California, the chemistry was stronger than before. "I promise you I'll never go away and leave you alone at Christmas time again," Kerry told me, and he never did.

Everything we did together was fun, including the dance lessons. We had a man that had been a drill sergeant in the army teach us. He drilled the men and women separately until we learned the step. Then he had us dance together. He had all the charm of a drill sergeant until he danced and then he was the most graceful man on the dance floor I'd ever seen.

My purpose is that they may be encouraged in heart and united in love, so that they may have the full riches of complete understanding, in order that they may know the mystery of God, namely, Christ, in whom are hidden all the treasures of wisdom and knowledge (Colossians 2:2,3).

❀ "The Best Decision I Ever Made"

When I met Kerry I had been going to the singles group at the Los Gatos Christian Church in Los Gatos, California. On Wednesday evenings they had a single's Bible class I attended. I told all my new friends about my witnessing to Kerry and I asked them to pray that he would come to know the Lord.

One evening after a date, we were sitting and discussing the Bible. I brought out the little booklet containing the four spiritual laws and was going over it with him. When we got to the page where it speaks about Jesus, he picked up the booklet and threw it on the table. Kerry pointed to the sentence saying He is the Only Way to God. "Why does it always come to this? What about all the good people in the world who have never heard of Jesus? What's going to happen to them?" Kerry sounded provoked.

I listened and assured him that it is those who believe in Jesus who will be with God in the life hereafter. He could see I didn't have a problem with that statement.

He asked another question. "What about God accepting me just as I am? How does that fit with, 'You are to be perfect just as your heavenly Father is perfect?' The whole concept seems hopeless to me," Kerry admitted.

"It would be hopeless without Jesus," I told him. "Without His blood sacrifice we would die in our sins. However, when He lives in us, it is His perfect life God sees."

"Gwen, you're the only Christian I ever met who sounds like you believe what you say. In fact your faith is what I find so intriguing about you."

"Why don't you go to church with me next Sunday? Our pastor will help you to see more clearly what the Bible teaches. He's starting a series of sermons through Hebrews."

"All right. I'll go once and see what it's like," Kerry agreed.

The following Wednesday at the single's Bible class I asked them to pray that the Holy Spirit would bring Kerry to the knowledge of the truth. Kerry attended the next Sunday when our pastor started his new series preaching through the entire book of Hebrews. On that first Sunday he was hooked. He never missed a service during that series, which lasted more than a year. Two of the members of the singles class were sitting behind us praying the Holy Spirit would help Kerry believe God's Word.

On Easter Sunday our service was held at the fair grounds in San Jose. Our pastor said, "We can choose to believe in Jesus and make Him our Lord and Savior, or we can try to be good enough on our own to get to heaven. It's a choice of God's will or your will. Will you believe in Jesus or in your own good works?"

Kerry jumped out of his seat and walked toward the pulpit to pray with the team of counselors assembled there.

"Where is Dad going?" his fourteen-year-old son, Matt, asked.

At first I wasn't sure, but then I saw him heading toward the pulpit. "I think he's going to dedicate his life to Jesus," I told Matt. "I'm going too," I told Matt. I wanted to recommit my life to Jesus. I followed Kerry.

A large pleasant man took us upstairs to a room above the auditorium where I heard Kerry pray to dedicate his life to following Jesus. "The moment I made the choice to believe God's Word, I knew the things that Gwen and our minister had been telling me were the truth," he witnessed. The following Sunday, Kerry was baptized. He said, "I want it all. I want to be on God's side."

I decided to become immersed with Kerry since the first time I was baptized I had been two weeks old and I'd been sprinkled.

I was thankful that Kerry believed in Jesus and we often prayed together.

Kerry composed the most beautiful prayers. Whenever we'd eat out, he prayed before meals no matter where we were. After we were married and went on cruises, he and I would pray together at the table of eight or ten people. On every occasion, one of the people at the table asked Kerry if he would pray for all of us. When he asked how the others felt about him praying, everyone at the table agreed, and the passengers often thanked him for his beautiful prayers. Sometimes I noticed people wiping away tears.

Later I told Kerry I had always prayed for a husband who would pray with me. Kerry became my prayer partner from the time he made the decision to follow Jesus. It no longer bothered Kerry that Jesus was the only way to God.

Over the twenty years after that Easter Sunday when Kerry made his decision to follow Jesus, he told me many times, "The decision I made on that Easter Sunday at the fairgrounds was the best decision anyone could ever make."

For it is by grace you have been saved, through faith—and this is not from yourselves, it is the gift of God—not by works, so that no one can boast (Ephesians 2:8).

🌼 Accepted for Who I Am

God had sent Kerry when I needed a friend. He found something in me he said he hadn't seen in anyone else. My absolute faith in God interested him.

Kerry accepted me as I was, which was having strange unexplainable reactions. When he first met me I was under a lot of stress, because I'd just started a new job after being divorced and not working away from home. I'd also gone through the death of both of my parents, so I had a great many adjustments to make.

My blood pressure went so high my doctor said, "I didn't think people could be up walking around with a blood pressure like yours." Doctors would check it three or four times before they would believe what they were seeing. I went to a doctor recommended by a lovely woman in my new church. He put me on an antidepressant and I felt so much better after one, he knew he was on the right track. Besides, my father experienced highs and then his emotional well-being would go very low. I noticed that when I took care of him, and figured that must have been where I'd gotten that tendency. Once the doctor got me stabilized it took two antidepressants a day to keep me on an even keel. The thing he couldn't seem to bring down was my blood pressure which was running stroke level.

It would be awhile before I found out what was keeping my body under such stress. Kerry felt it was some kind of chemical imbalance and he was close.

One day I had a glucose tolerance test after fasting. When I went in for the test I was feeling really good and my blood pressure was normal. Three hours after I'd taken a large drink containing glucose something very strange happened. Since the test took six hours, I brought stationery to write letters and I told Kerry I would be happy to hem his new suit slacks since I'd have so much time. It seemed the least I could do after he'd replaced my broken garbage disposal for me.

After writing some letters, I pulled out the slacks and let down the hem and measured the inseam. One leg measured six inches longer than the other one. It didn't make sense to me. I couldn't cut six inches off of one leg. They'd hung straight when I carried them in that morning and they belonged to a new suit. I simply couldn't believe my tape measure.

I started asking others taking the test why one leg was six inches longer than the other one, and they looked at the pants and could see they were the same length.

One of the men taking the test said, "She can't drive home like this. Somebody will have to drive her home."

At last, I knew it was what I had been eating or drinking that was making me see things in a strange way. I had plenty of witnesses who saw me change after the glucose drink. Later, I was given glucose during a surgery, and I thought the table was spinning around and around, and there were bright colored lights that became a blur because the doctors spun the operating table so often. Needless to say glucose had a very strange effect on me.

I worked for three C.P.A.s They knew something was wrong after I had written checks for one of their clients. They called me in and there were the checks all laid out that I had written the day before. I could hardly believe my eyes. It was my writing all right and I had written right through the middle of the lines on the checks. It had to be whatever I ate before I wrote those checks that caused me to think I was writing on top of the lines, when I wrote right through the middle of each line. That was the end of that job. The C.P.A.s said they felt the tax season coming up would be too much for me.

I recalled all the strange things that had happened to me lately. After dinner one evening, I got into the car and started driving to a Bible class Kerry and I had attended for three years, and I couldn't remember where to turn off. I went back and forth, up and down Blossom Hill Road, and I didn't have the slightest notion where the street was that I should turn off on. I finally stopped the car and prayed, asking God please to show me the right street to get to my Bible Class. After stopping to pray for God's help in getting there, I finally found the right street to get to my Bible Class, half an hour late.

At work a woman left a very precious art object for us to frame. We had the work order, but no art. Everyone in the store looked for three hours to find where I had put this woman's precious art, and at last it was found, placed in the matting material between the two colors of matting she'd selected. At the time it seemed the right place to put it.

Another day a man came into the art store smoking a pipe. That was before no smoking in stores. I waited on him. One minute I was talking to him and the next minute I inhaled some smoke and I didn't have the slightest idea what we'd been talking about.

Gasoline was something that bothered me so much, I had to get out of the car and wait at least half a block down the street until the car was filled with gas.

One day Kerry drove to the redwoods, and all at once I started crying for no reason at all. I continued crying as we walked through the redwoods, but once we left I was perfectly fine. It seems mildew or mold has a depressing effect on me. And yet I'd been in other redwood trees and not been affected.

One day my daughter, Terry, was making a pizza and I started crying. My son-in-law said, "Mom, I'm sorry if I said something that hurt your feelings."

"Wally, you didn't say anything that hurt my feelings," I answered, crying as if my heart would break. Kerry walked in at that point and said, "Where are your salts?"

I told him where they were and he went to get them saying, "She'll be all right once she gets the salts." I took the special salts the doctor had mixed for me to help stop allergic reactions, and within fifteen minutes I was back to normal. It was the yeast in the dough of the pizza Terry was making that brought on my tears. I can't eat pizza.

One day I opened the refrigerator and there sat my pin cushion. Sometimes I know the reason for my actions and other times I'm completely stumped. It could be anything I smelled, from a perfume to a protective coating they put on leather, to new carpet or insecticides that bothers me. I walked into a store one day through the insecticides, and I fainted. Someone picked me up and I got away from the smell and seemed all right. Then I wanted to go see a man about making some oak cabinets for me, and when I arrived at his place he was spraying some varnish on something new he'd built and I fainted again. I went to the emergency hospital and my blood pressure was half of what it usually was and they told me it was from shock to my system.

At least now I know I'll come out of the reaction if I just take a mixture of two parts potassium bicarbonate and one part calcium carbonate. There is no preparation in the drug store like this. My doctor had it ordered for me.

I actually used to think I was going out of my mind when a reaction started. Now I just pray God will see me through, and I go about my life praising Him for showing me how to live with my extreme intolerance to foods and smells. If I'd never had them there would have been many delicious foods I would never have learned to eat. I'm sure I would never have started serving lamb, and now lamb is the favorite meat of our guests, because they never fix it themselves. For awhile, when I had trouble finding foods to eat, I had frogs legs, rabbit, jicima—one of my favorites for salads that takes the place of apples. Anything new, I bought, because I couldn't have a reaction to it if I never ate it.

The reason people build an intolerance for foods is from eating them too often. Boxed foods are impossible for me to eat. I buy fresh fruits and vegetables and fish seems the easiest food for me to digest. I found monk fish that tasted just like lobster and I dipped it in butter, but I can't find it anymore. However, I can eat turkey, chicken, red meats, pork, and lamb. I simply cannot eat breaded foods or foods covered with a batter. Grains are all difficult, but rice and rye I can manage if I eat each only once a week and leave at least three days in between eating rye and rice. Wheat is out altogether. Grapes, apples, and pears are difficult for me to eat. Melons give me migraines if I eat them too often or eat too many varieties in a row. I became allergic to rutabagas when I used to slice them and fry them like potatoes. Corn is one vegetable I do not even try to eat. Cheese gives me migraines and anything with yeast or mushrooms is apt to make me depressed. Chocolate is fine once a week. Another thing I need to watch are medications. Those containing corn starch give me migraines.

One day my doctor asked, "Have you ever had asthma?"

My doctor tried me on a new high blood pressure medicine and I developed asthma. I started wheezing. "Have you had asthma before?" my doctor asked.

"No," I replied.

"I'm taking you off that new blood pressure medication. In rare cases it can cause asthma." My doctor was right. I've never had asthma again.

It is not only foods I have to watch, because shampoos, as well as other hair products, will give me large sores on my scalp if I use them too often. I build sensitivities very quickly, so I use a variety of products.

Kerry saw me through many reactions from the day he met me. Usually someone with so many reactions would scare a man off.

However, my faith in God intrigued Kerry more than my reactions disturbed him.

Consider it pure joy, my brothers, whenever you face trials of many kinds, because you know that the testing of your faith develops perseverance (James 1:2,3).

❀ An Unforgettable Wedding

My second wedding day was memorable, nothing like my first.

My first wedding had no friends, no flowers; only my mother, my father and my brother attended, because Harold wanted the fewest people possible.

When Kerry had learned about my first wedding he said, "We're going to have all our friends and relatives this time. I want you to have a grand wedding to remember."

The first thing Kerry did was to learn calligraphy so he could personally write out all our invitations by hand.

I bought a simple apricot colored floor-length dress and I wore an apricot net veil with white trim.

Kerry, in a tan tuxedo, was a handsome groom. Kerry's best man, his oldest son, David, also wore a tan tuxedo. My younger daughter, Cindy, was my bridesmaid. She wore a lovely long turquoise dress and she carried daisies and wore daisies in her hair. She preceded me down a long steep winding staircase lined with flowers and then it was my turn. I came down that long winding staircase and I proved I wasn't clumsy. I didn't even have to hold on. When I got to the first bend in the staircase I saw my handsome Kerry waiting for me, and my heart skipped a beat.

David walked forward to meet Cindy, and Kerry walked up to meet me.

We knelt on the kneeling bench, while our favorite male soloist from the choir sang the Lord's Prayer in his powerful voice. David Jones, our favorite younger pastor, presided at our wedding. He gave a sermonette based on Ephesians 5. First he spoke to me, "Gwen, Kerry is to be the

Gwen & Kerry
A Great Day—April 7, 1979

head of your family just as Christ is the head of the Church. You are to respect his authority in all things."

"And Kerry, you are to love Gwen as Christ loved the Church and gave Himself up for her. Remember you are to love Gwen the same way you love your own body. After all nobody hates his own body, but he feeds and cares for it the way Christ feeds and cares for the Church. When you love your wife, you love yourself."

In the next part of the ceremony, Kerry and I walked to a large candelabra with two smaller burning candles on the outside. We each took one of the smaller candles, and together we lit the one large candle in the middle and extinguished the two smaller candles, to indicate our two lives would no longer be separate but joined into one.

Next we recited our wedding vows.

The words, "Until death do us part," shattered my being. I convulsed into sobs. I recalled the first time I had taken those vows and I was suddenly grief stricken that I had failed to keep the promise I had made to God. Another problem struck me. By marrying Kerry while my first husband was still alive, I would be committing adultery according to the Bible. We had discussed this in a counseling session with the pastor before we were married. Even though, as he told us, that since both of our mates had remarried we were free to marry, I still felt convicted of sin. I was guilty of adultery and of not keeping my promise I made to God. If anyone noticed I was crying, they probably thought it was an emotional reaction, but it went much deeper. In those moments, I admitted to God I was a sinner and I couldn't stop crying because I knew I had grieved my heavenly Father. I repented of my sin right there at the altar.

God knew my heart and He forgave me.

It was as if a door opened to my heart and a huge eraser had come down from heaven and erased that sin from my heart and mind. I never suffered from guilt again about marrying Kerry. God wiped away my sin, as if it had never taken place. God knew the sorrow I felt for grieving Him and He stamped me "*Forgiven*" with the blood Jesus had shed on the cross. I had been convicted of sin and cleansed before more than a hundred people, and not one person in the audience had any idea of the real drama taking place in front of their very eyes. I never even told Kerry the battle that went on inside of me at the altar, because after the wedding the battle was over and Christ had already won the victory over my sin.

When Pastor said, "Now you may kiss the bride," Kerry gave me a long slow wonderful kiss that told me how happy he was that I was his bride. It didn't matter that everyone was watching. We wanted everyone to know we loved each other.

I heard a woman's voice shout, "All right!"

By the time we turned around to be introduced as Mr. and Mrs. Johnson, my composure was back, and tears of joy sprang to my eyes; and although my face was wet from my previous tears, I knew in my heart this marriage would last until death parted us.

This was our wedding day and we still had a reception to enjoy. Dorothy and Earl Pahnke, our shepherds at church, had offered to hold our reception in their beautiful home. We had met the Pahnkes because they had been elected shepherds over the people living in the Willow Glen district, where Kerry lived with his two sons; and when he received an invitation from the Pahnkes to attend the shepherding fellowship he asked me to go with him. The first time Dorothy met us she'd thought we were already a married couple. "Well, if you're not married you should be; you two look like you belong together," Dorothy said when she learned we were only dating.

She was right; we did belong together.

And sitting on Dorothy's lovely white lace covered table sat a gorgeous tiered wedding cake, quite different from the Hostess Cake wrapped in cellophane that my mother bought at the grocery store for my first wedding, and then forgot to serve.

Kerry's love for me and mine for him had gone into our preparation for our special day. Kerry's brother, David, and wife Monica, his sisters, Sandi and Barb, with husband, Bill, had come all the way from Minnesota, for the occasion. Three of Kerry's four step-daughters and his two sons were in attendance.

I'm glad I didn't realize that somehow we'd missed sending an invitation to my daughter, Terry. She and her family lived way out in Virginia, and I don't know how we missed letting her know we were getting married until after it was over. She really loved Kerry, and her daughter Tracy, eight at the time, told Kerry she wished he'd marry me because she wanted him for her grandpa. We did send them photographs of our wedding.

The photographs taken in Dorothy's yard were beautiful, but the one we both loved was of us coming out of the church and going down the stairs talking to each other, looking about twenty instead of fifty, which I was, and Kerry was forty-seven. We liked to talk and we never ran out of things to say to each other.

I had no idea what a wonderful marriage would follow that wedding. But after a week together I knew I would never tire of Kerry. Later, we became world travelers and everything we did together was exciting. God surely created us for each other because we understood one another so well from a human and spiritual viewpoint.

We had the ecstasy and the joy that all couples hope to find, only most couples look in the wrong places. We found life in Jesus Christ. We learned any other life is a poor imitation.

I felt God right in our midst. We drove His special love from us momentarily because our tempers flared, or because of another foolish reason, but we couldn't wait to tell each other we were sorry, and then we prayed for God's forgiveness and we'd be right back in His wonderful grace.

I am happy that I didn't change my mind at the altar. I would have missed the happiest twenty years of my life. Our lives were full of difficulties, but the joy we had in being together and knowing God was with us every step of the way, helped make our marriage special.

Set your minds on things above, not on earthly things. For you died, and your life is now hidden with Christ in God. When Christ, who is your life, appears, then you also will appear with him in glory (Colossians 3:2-4).

❀ A Valentine Message

On the first Valentine's Day after our marriage, Kerry gave me a beautiful valentine with a message at the bottom. "Dear Gwen, you are visible proof of God's love for me, in that while I was denying Him, He plucked me up one night and brought me to you at the Parents Without Partners meeting, entirely against my own desire."

When I asked Kerry what he meant, he explained he was referring to what had happened to him the day before we first met. He'd gone with Diane, a woman adjuster, to make a settlement with one of his company's insured, who was not happy with the amount of the settlement they had brought to her. She'd become angry and attacked both of them.

"Our insured grabbed the young woman adjuster and scratched her face," Kerry told me. "I stepped in between Diane and the powerfully built woman, and she turned on me. She grabbed me and started beating me about the face, neck, and shoulders. I knew I'd be in deep trouble if I pushed or hit this woman. I managed to work my way back to my car with the woman hitting me and swearing at us. All the way to my car she shrieked all kinds of filthy words." Kerry said he managed to stay between Diane and the insured. "That woman was still swearing and shaking her fist at us when we drove off."

He'd driven to the nearest hospital where they treated Diane's scratches. The next stop was the police station where they filed a report. Later, Diane won a settlement for her injuries.

By the time Kerry arrived home he just wanted to sit down and rest. It had been a very upsetting day. He really didn't want to see anyone. He had thought about going to the Parents without Partners meeting that night before this all happened.

"I was sitting there in my chair resting and it was as if someone pulled me up out of the chair and pushed me out of my front door to attend that meeting. Now I know it was God's Holy Spirit pushing me out the door so I would be present at that meeting where I first met you," Kerry told me.

"What a testimony to the way God works in our lives. I'm surprised you didn't tell me this before," I told Kerry.

He finished writing on my Valentine, "I live my life in gratitude to Jesus Christ because you obeyed Him and spoke His message of life to me. I love you, bless you, and thank you for blessing me and my family by reflecting Christ's Spirit to us."

Because I introduced Kerry to his Savior and Lord, he had a very special love for me. His love was obvious in the way he looked at me, the way he helped me up from the kneeling bench the day we were married, and the way he never stopped thanking me for loving him.

Kerry was the first person in my life who really loved me unconditionally. Because of his love, I felt it was possible for God to love me, too. Kerry made me feel special, and he let me know that, to him, I was the most important human being on earth.

I pray that you, being rooted and established in love, may have power, to grasp how wide and long and high and deep is the love of Christ, and to know this love that surpasses knowledge—that you may be filled to the measure of all the fullness of God (Ephesians 3:17b-19).

🌸 My Rest in the Storms of Life

One year after Kerry and I married, we took a trip and on the way we stopped at the Badlands in South Dakota. Standing there reading a sign, I was stirred in my imagination. It read: A Battle Is Raging Here, The Battle Between the Forces of Nature.

Torrential rains, turbulent winds, and the driving snows of winter have fashioned jagged spires and knife-edged ridges of sandstone. At the same time, erosion is working to destroy this wild and scenic beauty.

How like my own life, I thought, as I viewed the spectacular cliffs. Many of my personal storms, I now realized, were merely winds of my own impatience and discontent. I'd selfishly wanted my own way. I thought my circumstances must change or that someone in my life needed to change to satisfy me.

God used each self-centered storm to bring me closer to the truth that I was the one who needed to change. I was aware that the One who shaped the Badlands, could mold me through the storms in my life to make me more and more like Jesus.

Storms of Worry and Anxiety

Persistent worry and anxiety hammered away at my life like flurries of hail. As hail chipped hollowed impressions into the layers of rock which form the Badland Buttes, so continuous worry and anxiety chipped away my mental and emotional well-being, causing me periods of unrest, indecision, and ultimately depression.

Though I taught my Sunday School students that they needed to place their trust in the Lord, I had not learned to entirely rely on Him in every circumstance. I placed myself in God's care for surgeries and the big problems of life that I knew I couldn't handle, but the small everyday difficulties I tried to manage on my own.

I worried about the little perplexities of life until they often became the insurmountable problems I feared. I'd pray for God's help, but then I'd grab the problem back and try to work things out in my own way.

When living my way became too difficult for me to bear, I finally asked God to take over the control of my life. Following God's will brought me such peace and joy, I learned to reject my old ways of living and seek His direction for my life. My storms of worry and anxiety diminished and I felt a new freedom I'd never felt before.

Storms of Unconfessed Sin

A habit pattern of recalling unkind words spoken to me as a child, worked like erosion, whittling away at my peace and contentment. Born in the Great Depression, I had been told repeatedly, "The last thing we needed when you were born was another baby." By reviewing this statement and other hurtful remarks, I wallowed in unforgiveness and self-pity. I refused to take responsibility for my actions by continually blaming my mother's rejection and her unkind words for the difficulties I encountered.

Then I remembered that Jesus had already paid for my mother's hurtful remarks and the other injustices I felt I'd been forced to endure. When He died on the cross, He had also paid for my sins of unforgiveness and self-pity and guilt. But I was still carrying the burden of my sin. My shoulders were stooped from bearing such a heavy load.

I reminded myself that Jesus was sent to take away the burden of sins. I simply needed to unload them and give them to Him.

I searched out every hurtful remark buried in the hidden recesses of my mind. I grabbed the pile of hurtful comments and forgave each person who had hurt me, asking God to cleanse their remarks from my memory. No more would mere words keep me from enjoying the forgiveness Jesus offered me as a free gift.

Once my sins of unforgiveness and self-pity and the guilt they created were confronted, confessed, and exposed to the light of Christ's sacrifice, God forgave all my sins and my guilt was gone!

Storms of a Critical Spirit

I had been helping an elderly woman who had a negative and critical spirit. I saw how her bitterness had estranged her children and friends. Her negative attitude brought her pain, loneliness, and misery. When my son-in-law told me that everything I'd said since he'd come home for a visit was negative, I paid attention. I knew I must deal with my negative thinking. I asked God to help me change my complaints into praising Him for His goodness, my fault-finding into constructive criticism, and my negative statements into positive ones.

However, like slipping on the ice and snow of winter in the Badlands, I still occasionally slip back into my old habits of complaining and criticizing myself and others. God's Spirit reminds me I am loved in spite of my imperfections. I asked the Lord to give me Jesus' special love and acceptance for the person I have criticized, so I can love him or her exactly as He loves and accepts me in spite of all my faults and sins.

Storms of Illness

As the torrential rains hit repeatedly in the Badlands, so the storms of illness hit repeatedly throughout my life. Weaknesses manifested themselves in nearly every area of my body, causing infections to rage and pain to dominate my life. My primary physician, after sending me to four surgeons who found it necessary to operate during a period of five years asked me a strange question. "Were your father and mother related?"

When I told him they had not been related he looked me straight in the eye and said: "You have too many weaknesses. The seed responsible for your birth should never have been fertilized."

I cried out in pain, despairing in my weaknesses. My strength evaporated. Finally in my late forties I pleaded, "Lord God, please let Jesus come live His holy life in and through me."

And Jesus became my strength in times of weakness and my hiding place in every storm.

Storms of Loss

Deaths of loved ones in my life were as unforeseen as bolts of lightning flashing across the sky in the Badlands. The deaths of my baby sister and my grandmother struck without warning. One day my mother was alive and well, the next day her life on earth had ended. My father's death followed not long after my mother's. The storms of loss were taking their toll.

The loss of three consecutive jobs struck abruptly, leaving me stunned—much like hearing the crash of thunder without any other warning of impending storm.

And yet God used these unwelcomed losses to help me grow as a person and to teach me to give Jesus not only my sins to bear, but also my griefs and heartaches as well. It was during these difficult times that my faith in Jesus' power for my life grew.

Understanding that God directs my steps as Christ lives in me, has saved me from having to speculate or worry about what happens. Since nothing happens without God's knowledge, I must walk by faith, trusting that He knows what is best for my life. I've learned to thank and praise Him in all things, even in the midst of problems and pain, because I know He is trustworthy. He turns problems into blessings and pain into joy.

The promise of finding rest in life's storms is available to everyone. Jesus entreatingly invites: *"Come unto Me, all who are weary and heavy burdened and I will give you rest."*

If the battle between the forces of nature in the Badlands of South Dakota can bring about such radical changes, how much more is Jesus' presence in my life able to transform me when I am willing to yield my will to His!

Do not conform any longer to the pattern of this world, but be transformed by the renewing of your mind. Then you will be able to test and approve what God's will is—His good, pleasing, and perfect will (Romans 12:2).

*Published as "Our Rest in the Storms of Life" in *Power for Living*, 07/22/90, a Scripture Press Publication.

11

Learning to Listen to Children

Jesus said, "Let the little children come to me, and do not hinder them, for the kingdom of heaven belongs to such as these" (Matthew 19:14).

 Open Pool—Open Hearts

 A Joyful Surprise

 Still Friends

 If All Else Fails—Try Love

 Our Grandchildren's Heritage

 What a Difference Prayer Makes

"Which of you fathers, if your son asks for a fish, will give him a snake instead? Or if he asks for an egg, will give him a scorpion? If you then... know how to give good gifts to your children, how much more will your Father in heaven give the Holy Spirit to those who ask him!" (Luke 11:11).

❀ Open Pool—Open Hearts

When I first glimpsed the beautiful pool area behind our new home, I pictured my husband and myself enjoying long leisurely afternoons in our pool—but God had other plans! I never dreamed it would completely change our lives.

I certainly never imagined our pool teeming with kids of all sizes, shapes, and races, but that's exactly what happened. During the past twelve years, our backyard, with its small resting pool along with the large 20 x 40 foot pool, has become a learning center for all the neighborhood youth. Swimming starts at 3:00, on week days, from April through October, closing only for vacations.

It all began one morning when we asked the kids next door if they wanted to swim. They asked their friends and before I realized it, we had an ongoing pool party that has become a neighborhood mission. Besides having a place to learn how to swim, the children know this is one place where they and their friends are accepted, regardless of their background.

One day my neighbor from across the street came over to watch her two children swim. "Did you know there are five ethnic groups represented in your resting pool alone?" she asked.

I glanced over and saw five teenage girls busily chatting, enjoying the warmer water.

Marvat, an Arabic girl with olive skin and black hair came from Israel with her parents. Andrea was Spanish-American. Sandi, an African-American, was visiting with Billy and Monica. Meredith, an extremely fair-skinned Scandinavian, was deep in conversation with Pearl, her lovely Japanese friend.

I decided to ask the kids swimming in the large pool about their backgrounds. On that particular day we had Puerto Rican, English, French, German, Scottish, Polish, and Jewish backgrounds represented. Summer after summer, young people with all types of backgrounds enjoy swimming together and learning about God's love.

Clay was only four when he first came to swim. He did all sorts of things to get attention. He often used God's name in the wrong way. I told him, "If you want to swim in my pool you must stop using God's name as a swear word." I explained why it was wrong. The next time he did it, I asked him to leave. When he refused, I picked him up bodily and put him outside our fence.

His lower lip jutted out in a pout and he looked as if he were about to cry. "Can't I ever come back and swim anymore?" he asked.

"Yes, you may come again tomorrow," I told him. "But if you use God's name in the wrong way, you'll have to leave again. Remember, Clay, I still love *you*. It's your words and actions that make me unhappy."

Several more times it became necessary to snatch Clay from the pool, but now he's a tall handsome eighteen-year-old and he's invited Jesus into his life. Clay was in the first group of swimmers I'd taken to Vacation Bible School at our church. Before I started backyard Bible Clubs, all the kids crammed into our car and I'd take them to church, where I stayed and taught a class. The group of youth wanting to go became so large that the church sent a bus to my house to pick them up.

About eight years ago our church introduced Backyard Bible Clubs. I agreed to hold one and teach. This proved highly successful because kids who would never get to go to church could hear about Jesus. The first year more than twenty kids attended, the second more than thirty, and the third more than forty children enrolled for the week. Kids got to swim after the class was over once they said their Bible verse for the day.

Kathy came in her van with a group of kids from her neighborhood along with her two sons. She taught the songs, then I taught the lesson; Becky did a puppet show after the lesson and she taught crafts. And after my husband retired, he told them the missionary story.

Sometimes kids asked questions for half an hour after the lesson. "It's as if they're starved to hear more about God's Word," one helper remarked. Young people have a great yearning to know about God. Best of all, since I started having Backyard Bible Clubs, many of the youngsters have received Jesus as their Savior from sin and made Him Lord over their lives. One year alone, thirteen children prayed to receive Jesus.

I can't think of a better way to express Christ's love to children than to provide a neighborhood swimming pool for them to enjoy each summer. I'd like to encourage any of you who have pools to do the same. And if you don't have a pool, have the neighborhood children over to teach them to sew, whittle, make things, play an instrument, or teach and play board games with them. You will learn how delightful children are, and you can tell them about God while you're working with them.

More than anything, kids need someone to listen to them. They want and need praise, but not phony praise, because they know the difference. If they perform a great dive, I praise them, but when they mess up I also tell them, "That was a real belly flop." They know, then, they can trust me for a fair assessment. Without older adults caring about them, kids get into trouble, because often no adult is taking the time to listen to them and care about what they're doing. Being locked up may seem better than the indifference they get at home.

Grandmothers, if you aren't playing games or doing things with your grandchildren you're missing out on a wonderful time. Children can be so creative. I love to watch them do little skits on the diving board, using me as a judge to score their performances. They figure out all sorts of ways to fall or jump from the diving board; some are hilarious!

If you think you're too old to work with kids, that may be an excuse. I'm sixty-nine and I feel younger every year since I've been swimming with kids. Their humor and unpredictability keep me young.

I know God has blessed us in many ways the past fifteen years since we opened our pool to the neighborhood kids. Don't let your health stand in the way. My husband has cancer and pulmonary fibrosis, and he loves watching and talking with the kids, and it takes his mind off his problems and gives him other things to enjoy. I feel happier and healthier when I play with the younger crowd. Opening our pool has opened our hearts to new levels of joy and hope and celebration.

Command them to do good, to be rich in good deeds, and to be generous and willing to share. In this way they will lay up treasure for themselves as a firm foundation for the coming age, so that they may take hold of the life that is truly life (1 Timothy 6:18-19).

*In l995, "Open Pool—Open Hearts" was purchased by *Wesleyan Woman* for their 1996 Winter edition, published by Wesleyan Women International of the Wesleyan Church. Previously it appeared in a slightly different form as "Pool Party," in *Power for Living*, June 28, 1992, published by Scripture Press. It appeared in *ALIVE!*, August, 1993 as "C'Mon In! The Water's Fine," published by Christian Senior Fellowship, Inc.

❀ A Joyful Surprise

"Is anyone ready to talk to me about receiving Jesus as their Lord and Savior?" I asked during a week-long Vacation Bible Club at my home. Three hands shot into the air.

Since I taught the lesson, I would speak individually with each child who raised a hand. Little seven-year-old Sarah was the first child I took aside while my helpers started the other children on crafts.

My little granddaughter, Sita, slipped into the room while I was talking to Sarah. She sat quietly within hearing distance.

I explained to Sarah that since God is holy, He cannot stand sin in His presence. "The only way we can get close to Him is through Jesus, because He lived a life free from sin. When He died on the cross, He paid for the bad things we do and the good we fail to do," I told Sarah.

Sarah sat listening intently.

"We need to feel sorry for those things we do that displease God and ask His forgiveness. Then by praying for Jesus to come live His life in and through us as our Savior from sin, and as the Lord over our lives, we can come close to God and call Him our heavenly Father."

Sarah nodded and smiled.

"When we make Jesus Lord, it means doing things His way instead of our way. It means learning what God's will is and then doing it," I told her.

"Now are you ready to pray and ask Jesus to forgive your sins and become Lord over your life?" I asked.

She looked up at me through her beautiful azure blue eyes and said, "No!"

I sat stunned.

"I'm ready," a little voice piped up from across the room. My granddaughter Sita jumped up, walked over, and stood in front of me. "Grandma, I'm sorry for the bad things I've done. Can I pray and ask Jesus to come live in me?"

"Oh, sweetheart, if you're ready you sure can."

I asked Sarah to join the rest of the kids who were working on crafts. I knew I would be speaking with her again later.

My heart had leaped for joy when I learned Sita wanted to ask Jesus into her life. I wanted to be certain, however, that she understood the meaning of this decision, since she was not yet five.

I went over every point again. She listened, engrossed in everything I told her and in the questions I asked. Her answers and comments indicated she knew exactly what she was doing.

Then she bowed her head and asked God to forgive her for all the bad things she had done and the loving things she had failed to do.

"Heavenly Father," she continued to pray, "Please let Jesus come live in me so I will be able to make you happy. Help me to make Jesus Lord over my life. Amen."

She looked up at me through her sparkling brown eyes and proclaimed, "Now, I have Jesus living in my heart."

I grabbed her up in my arms and hugged her. "Yes, you do—and don't ever forget that."

About a week later, Sita became involved in an angry argument with her friend Jeannine. Suddenly she stopped and asked her friend to bow her head while she prayed. She told God she knew that her arguing did not make Him happy and asked His forgiveness. Then she asked her friend to forgive her, too, saying she was sorry.

The two girls happily returned to playing together. My daughter called me to relate this action.

I had felt little Sita might be too young for my Bible Club, but God showed me once again His ways are beyond my understanding. Although Sarah did not pray to receive Jesus at this time, she did later. God used her to open the way for my granddaughter, Sita, to accept His plan of salvation. What a joyful surprise!

Jesus took a little child and had him stand among them. Taking him in his arms, he said to them, "Whoever welcomes one of these little children in my name welcomes me; and whoever welcomes me does not welcome me but the one who sent me" (Mark 9:36-37).

*"A Joyful Surprise" appeared in *Living with Children* in 1992. Later it was published in *Live*, December, 1993.

❀ Still Friends

"Grandma, Grandma! Miles won't let me wear his new underwater goggles. I don't want to play with him any more," my little six-year-old grandson told me one day while we were swimming in the pool together.

"Are you telling me that you don't want to play with Miles just because he won't lend you his goggles?" I asked, startled by what I'd just heard.

"That's right. I don't want to play with him if he won't let me try his goggles."

"Aren't you making this way too important, J.D.?"

I called Miles. "Please come here, I want to talk to you and J.D. together." Miles swam over to where J.D. and I were standing. Adorable, curly headed six-year-old Miles stood eyeing me with a quizzical expression.

"Now J.D., if wearing Miles underwater glasses is more important than having Miles for a friend, I'm afraid you may not keep many friends. From what I've seen of those types of goggles, they don't work very well and they get so much water in them you can barely see anyway. They'll be worn out before long. What's more important, to have Miles' friendship, which could last a lifetime, or wearing glasses that probably will be no good six months from now?"

J.D.'s lower lip trembled and his mouth turned down in the corners. "Well, I guess having Miles for a friend is more important," he finally managed to stammer.

Then I looked at Miles. "Miles, your parents bought these goggles for you and you have every right not to let J.D. use them. You can pick the times you want to let other kids borrow them or you can choose not to lend them at all. That's your choice. However, whatever you put into a friendship is what you'll get back. If you share with others, they'll share with you. The Bible tells us what we give in life is what we can expect to get back." Miles had attended at least three of my Backyard Bible Clubs.

Then I looked at both of the boys. "Each of you should think not only of your own interests, but also the interests of others."

"Is lending J.D. my goggles looking out for his interests?" Miles asked.

"I think it is. He's certainly interested in seeing if your glasses work, isn't he?"

Miles took off his glasses and handed them to J.D. "Here, J.D. But when I ask for them back, I want you to give them to me. That's why I hate to loan you stuff. You never want to give things back."

"All right," J.D. answered joyfully, looking at the goggles in his hand. "I promise to give them back whenever you ask."

"All right! Give them back *now*!" Miles stated.

"Aw, Grandma, do I have to? I haven't even got to wear them yet."

"What did you promise?" I asked J.D.

"To give them back when he asked me," J.D. admitted.

J.D. held the glasses out looking as if he were about to cry.

"I was just kidding," Miles said, swimming away with a big grin on his face.

J.D. quickly put the goggles on and adjusted the strap in the back, before Miles could change his mind again. He plunged under the water to try them out.

Yes, they're still friends and play together whenever J.D. comes to visit me.

Each of you should look not only to your own interests, but also to the interests of others (Philippians 2:4).

✿ If All Else Fails—Try Love

"How will we ever get through our Friday night musical with eight little gangster-type hoodlums?" I wondered. The "hoodlums" were among nearly fifty children in the combined fourth through sixth grades of our Vacation Bible School. These children had come from twenty-five different schools and represented many different backgrounds.

The eight boys, all dressed in black, were brought by a missionary working on the east side. They formed a type of "gang." All the other kids were a little afraid of them and they kept their distance, careful not to annoy them in any way.

It was Thursday, and we'd gathered all the children from kindergarten through sixth grade, to rehearse the play planned for parents at the close of our V.B.S. on Friday evening. The "Terrible Eight" were conducting themselves as usual.

During the week their teachers had coaxed, exhorted, threatened, and even pleaded for their attention, with little success. They had chased away four teachers, two of them men. Only the lead teacher and I had stuck it out.

Now we were trying to get them through a rehearsal. George was slipping down the stairs of the choir loft on his back while Joe urged him on, and the rest of the pack hooted. George and Joe were the acknowledged leaders.

A singer from the adult choir hauled George off the stairs and plunked him down beside me. *What am I going to do?* I wondered, breathing a desperate prayer for help.

I had to act fast so I placed my arm around George's waist and hugged him. He responded by snuggling closer. With my left arm around George, I reached out with my right arm and encircled Joe's waist. Again I encountered no attempt to pull away.

When it was time for the children to perform, I watched with admiration, and a bit of shock, as Joe stood on the top step of the choir loft and sang out every word loud and clear. The voices of the "Terrible Eight" added greatly to the chorus.

Their old habits didn't disappear entirely. But their leaders, who had apparently been subdued by my hugs, kept the gang under control.

On the evening of the actual performance, when I walked to the choir loft, George put his arm around my shoulders and said, "You look beautiful tonight." As the other seven filed in, he asked each one, "Doesn't she look beautiful tonight." None dared to contradict him.

Because I'd strained my knee from all the activity of the week, I wore an elastic support on my knee. George made sure I was comfortably seated. "You don't have to chase anyone tonight," he promised. "Sit still and rest."

George attentively watched over me throughout the evening, his eyes reflecting his love and concern. I was reminded of Jesus' command: *"Love each other"* (John 15:17). I decided I'd follow that command in the future—before all else fails.

Now that you have purified yourselves by obeying the truth so that you have sincere love for your brothers, love one another deeply, from the heart (1 Peter 1:22).

*This article appeared in *Power for Living,* 1992, June/July/August issue.

❀ Our Grandchildren's Heritage

My husband, Kerry, and I had brought Adam, our eleven-year-old grandson, to talk to the children's minister prior to his baptism. Pastor Deming asked Adam when he decided he wanted to know God personally.

Adam answered, "When I was three or four years old, sitting in my grandparents' truck, Grandma drove up over a hill and the street divided into three roads. Grandma said, 'I don't know which way to go. At least one of these roads leads out of town, and I might have trouble finding my way back.' Then I heard her say, 'God, I don't know which way to go. Please show me the right way.' God showed Grandma the right way and she thanked Him."

She told me, "Whenever you don't know which way to turn, always ask God and He'll show you." I thought, "Wow! I've got to know this God-fellow."

I sat stunned. He was so little when that happened I couldn't believe he'd remembered. "Adam, I think Pastor Deming wants to know when you prayed for Jesus to come live in your heart."

"Oh. That was when I was around eight. At one of my grandmother's Backyard Bible Clubs she taught the lesson about how Adam and Eve sinned. At the end of the lesson she asked if anyone would like to ask Jesus into their lives to forgive their sins. I raised my hand. Later that evening Grandpa and Grandma talked to me about sin. They told me God wants me to be sorry for those things I do to displease Him, and He wants me to confess each sin and ask Him for forgiveness. I prayed, thanking Jesus for shedding His blood to save me from my sins. I named the bad things I had done, and I asked Jesus to forgive me and become Lord over my life, and come live in my heart and show me how to keep from sinning, and how to live His way."

"What does it mean to make Jesus Lord of your life?" Pastor Deming asked.

"When you make Jesus Lord that means He's the boss and you do things His way," Adam answered.

The very next Sunday, Adam and his sister Amberly were baptized. On the way home we asked Adam and Amberly if they felt any different after being baptized.

"Yes, I do," Adam spoke up. "I knew I wanted Jesus to be my Lord and Savior. Now, I know He'll take care of me, cherish me, and cleanse me of my sin. Now that I'm baptized I feel more confident. I know who I am and I know I'm going to heaven."

Amberly decided after Adam talked with the pastor, that she wanted to be baptized with her brother. She felt much more secure and happier after she was baptized, too. What joy filled our hearts to hear how happy these two children were to be baptized. Adam is a good role model for his two younger sisters and for the younger children that are in my Backyard Bible Clubs.

There is an ingredient in our lives that few people have—it is the joy of the Lord. Our grandchildren and neighborhood kids love to spend time with us learning more about Jesus. We encourage them to become all that God wants them to be. We teach the children by creating an open, sharing, listening, and forgiving atmosphere for them. We pray God's Holy Spirit will teach our twenty grandchildren to instinctively know right from wrong and that He will guide them to make right decisions. They need to know God's Word so they will seek His will in everything.

I believe that our lives are the best way to influence our grandchildren, nieces, nephews, and the children in our neighborhood. We can show that God does make a difference. It's our actions which show whether or not we really believe in God. We teach by showing them God is the center of our existence. This assures our grandchildren that having God as the center of life produces a happier existence.

My husband has cancer and pulmonary fibrosis but our twenty grandchildren don't see him sitting and moping about his lot. No, he plays with his grandchildren. In the past he swam with them, and he's happy and loving. He lets them know He believes in Jesus and he's not afraid to die, because when he does, he'll be with God the Father and Jesus Christ.

I also show the kids by my attitude that I believe in God. I don't sit around worrying about their grandpa. Our grandchildren know they can count on us. We let them know they are loved, and how much they mean to us. Our home is full of laughter and joy.

We consider each Sunday as our day with the grandchildren who live nearby. First we attend Sunday School and church. Afterward we have fun eating out. In the summer we swim in our pool and in the winter we play board games, or take them to the playground. We travel to see and play with those grandchildren who are out of town.

People ask all the time what makes these children so full of laughter and joy? We know it is because their faith is real!

The heritage we want to leave our grandchildren is our love for Jesus, our positive faith in Him, the knowledge of right and wrong. They know our earthly bodies will die, but they are comforted by knowing we will all be reunited in heaven, to enjoy our gift of everlasting life in the glorious presence of our living Lord.

Children's children are a crown to the aged, and parents are the pride of their children (Proverbs 17:6).

*This was published in the *Wesleyan Woman*, Spring 2000, issue 6.

❀ What a Difference Prayer Makes

When I teach my Backyard Bible Clubs I am particularly pleased that the children remain quiet and listen attentively when I teach.

One day I noticed the children squirming and they all seemed restless. One child got up from the floor and made a commotion while getting seated in another area.

Natalie held up her hand.

"Yes, Natalie, did you want to share something?" I asked.

"Yes, I wondered what was happening here today. Why are all the kids so restless?"

"I wondered the same thing," I answered.

"Oh, Mrs. Johnson, I know what's been happening," Natalie said suddenly.

"Please tell me what's happening."

"Well, Mrs. Johnson, you forgot to pray before we started the lesson today. That's what's wrong."

"Is that true? Did I forget to pray before I started teaching?" I asked the young people. They sat and thought a minute and then they all agreed with Natalie. I had not prayed before the lesson started.

"No wonder you were all reacting so differently today. Natalie's right. We need to pray before we discuss God's Word. Bow your heads for a prayer, and we'll start over again." All of the children bowed their heads and I prayed for God's Spirit to work in them as I taught the lesson, and I thanked God's Holy Spirit for reminding Natalie I hadn't prayed before I started teaching.

This time the children were quiet and listened respectfully as I taught the lesson. What a difference a prayer made.

"If you believe, you will receive whatever you ask for in prayer" (Matthew 21:22).

12

Breaking the Chains of Unforgiveness

Be kind and compassionate to one another,
forgiving each other, just as in Christ God
forgave you (Ephesians 4:32).

 The Lie I Never Told

 A Pertinent Question about Forgiveness

 "Mom, Can You Forgive Me?"

For he has rescued us from the dominion of darkness
and brought us into the kingdom of the Son he loves,
in whom we have redemption, the forgiveness of sins
(Colossians 1:13,14).

❀ The Lie I Never Told

"Please forgive me, Gwennie." My brother stood with his arms wrapped around me, hugging me to him.

We were shedding tears about an incident which had occurred more than forty years earlier. My brother, then seventeen, had asked me to help him indulge in a fantasy of his that I knew to be wrong. I was only fifteen and had refused, but I still carried the emotional scars from that incident.

In my heart I'd forgiven my brother for what he'd asked, but I'd been unforgiving toward my mother who refused to believe me when I reported the episode.

I could still hear my mom telling me, "Henry would never ask such a thing. I don't know why you're saying this."

"Go ask Henry. I don't think he'd lie to you."

"I'll do no such thing. I don't know why you're lying to me."

Those words had gone over and over in my mind until I wondered if maybe I had made the whole thing up.

My mother's judgmental reaction had built a barrier between my brother and me, and I never again confided in my mother. The whole matter could have been cleared up and my mother could have prevented painful emotional scars if she had just called my brother in and questioned him when I reported the incident.

My brother had gone into the service at eighteen, and then I got married a year later and moved to California, so it had been years since we'd seen each other. He dropped by to see me while he was visiting in California and during a discussion he'd said, "Gwennie, it sounds as if we had two different mothers."

"We did," I'd blurted out. "Mother always believed you, but she wouldn't believe me, especially when I told her what you asked of me that day."

My brother looked up at me shocked. "You told Mom? Oh, Gwennie, please forgive me. Forgive me for what I asked that day." It was then my brother wrapped his arms around me. "Gwennie, years ago I asked God to forgive me for what I asked you that day, but I never thought about asking you to forgive me."

I burst into tears.

"I'm sorry, I never meant to hurt you so much. I never knew you'd told Mom." Now my brother was crying, too.

However, my brother had cleared me of a lie I'd never told. In the presence of his wife, he acknowledged that what I remembered of that event from so many years before was true. When my brother asked me to forgive him, I could say, "Yes, I do forgive you," and I meant it. All the anger I'd felt against my older brother was gone. After all, he had never asked me to do anything improper like that again.

The day my brother confessed was the day I started healing. It was necessary for me to let go of the unforgiveness I'd held against my mother all those years. Carrying unforgiveness and the guilt of being accused of lying about the incident left me feeling unworthy to accept God's love.

Although going through this brought Jesus even closer, because He was the only one I could confide in, it did make it hard for me to believe He could love me. My mother's accusation made me wonder if God could really love the liar I'd been accused of being. After all, there were even moments when I began to wonder if I could have made the whole episode up.

However, when Henry told me, "Sometimes people aren't cured of an illness because they are holding unforgiveness in their hearts," I became acutely aware that God's Holy Spirit meant that message for me. Could the unforgiveness I held toward my mother be the reason I suffered from so many illnesses?

That night after I prayed asking for God's help, I started searching the dark hollows of my mind and examining my thought patterns. I found words spoken by my mother that I had never forgiven. The one I heard the most often was: "Another baby was the last thing we wanted when you were born." I hadn't asked to be born, and hearing those words over and over, hurt. Bringing a report card home with all "Excellent" marks only to be told, "They should see how dumb you are at home; they'd never give you those grades," created another sore spot. I'd worked so hard for those grades and I wanted some recognition.

I discovered unforgiven hurts such as these fastening themselves to the unswept corners of my mind, hindering God's peace and joy in my life. I remembered that, as a small child, I had started the habit of bringing up "injustices" I suffered so I could feel sorry for myself. And even though I paraded to others the terrible things my mother had said, I was still getting the attention I wanted, for I enjoyed hearing my friends say, "Those were dreadful things for your mother to say to you!"

By repeating these negative things, I could blame my mother for my actions. "It's no wonder I'm like I am; after all, my mother said all these mean things to me." By not forgiving my mother for her statements, I was preventing myself from maturing into a responsible adult, and I was impairing my Christian witness.

I knew I had to ask God to forgive me for the unforgiveness I'd carried toward my mother for more than forty years. I needed to wipe that event and other times of unfair treatment from my memory, and stamp it with *Forgiven*, the way Jesus had done for me when He died for my sins.

What relief and peace it brought me when I asked God to forgive me for my bad feelings toward my mother and for the anger I felt toward Henry for putting me through such an unpleasant situation. At last I'd found the key to unlock the chains of sin and guilt in my life.

When I was with my brother three days before he died, I felt nothing but love and admiration for the remarkable way he had taught God's Word to the inmates in prisons for years, and for how he had carried that ministry through until the end of his life. He'd died a happy man, with a family who loved and admired him. Because of Henry's faithful prison ministry, many prisoners had found Jesus and had inherited eternal life.

I was thankful that through Henry's statement about unforgiveness he'd awakened me to the truth that had kept me miserable. My unforgiveness had not hurt my mother, but it had done terrible damage to me and to my relationship to God.

"For if you forgive men when they sin against you, your heavenly Father will also forgive you. But if you do not forgive men their sins, your Father will not forgive your sins" (Matthew 6 14-15).

❀ A Pertinent Question about Forgiveness

One Sunday, a long distance phone call delayed my husband and me from arriving at church on time. Coming late we found a woman crying. The greeters out front seemed embarrassed by her presence.

I put my arms around her. When her sobbing quieted, I asked what was wrong.

"My husband came to pick up our son after he'd attended Sunday School and I'd attended the first service." Her voice quivered as she spoke. "Our son was late in getting to the car. My husband said he was leaving without him. Jimmy was too young to get home by himself. I refused to get into the car without our son. My husband drove off and left us."

"Why don't we pray about it?" I prayed her husband would calm down and come back to pick them up, and I thanked God for hearing our prayer.

The woman quieted down. Soon after the prayer, her husband drove back into the parking lot. This time I went with the mother and son to the car.

"Hello!" I greeted her husband. "You know, one of the reasons we come to church is to hear about how Jesus died on the cross to forgive our sins. Since Jesus died to forgive us, don't you think you could forgive your son for being a little late, today?"

The man's face broke into a smile. "I guess that is a reasonable request."

The boy jumped into the car after his mother. I went on to church a little late, but happy I'd followed my heavenly Father's urging.

"Now I know why we were late this morning," Kerry said, when I told him later what had happened.

Not long afterward I saw this same man attending church with his wife.

An anxious heart weighs a man down, but a kind word cheers him up (Proverbs 12:25).

✿ "Mom, Can You Forgive Me?"

"Mom, Mom, are you OK?" It was my daughter's voice.

I groped around in total darkness, feeling as if a mule had kicked me in the stomach. I couldn't breathe. A surge of agonizing pain stabbed my right arm and it felt twice its normal size. When at last I caught my breath, the only answer I could get out was, "No!"

"Mom, where are you?" Cindy's voice sounded distant.

My hand touched a water ski, and for the first time I realized we were trapped under our ski boat.

My mind raced as I tried to focus on what had happened.

Only moments before, Cindy had been driving our boat, towing her step-brother, Matt, on skis.

I had been uncomfortable being in the boat with Cindy after yet another argument we'd had earlier. So I was concentrating on Matt skiing back and forth over the boat's wake.

Cindy had turned her head to watch her brother ski. She had been unaware of a jagged rock just beneath the water. The instant she looked around, the boat had turned slightly toward the shore. The sharp rock had caught the bow, ripping through the fiberglass. When the boat's propeller struck the rock we had been hurtled into the water.

The boat had flipped on top of us.

Suddenly, a ray of light revealed Matt's friend, Terry, lifting the boat and squirming out. Then, he held it up for me to crawl to safety. The bright afternoon sun stung my eyes as I emerged from the darkness. Matt, free of his skis, was there to welcome me. He led me to some rocks, where I sat down as Terry returned to rescue Cindy.

When she sat down on rocks directly in front of me, Cindy sobbed. "First I damage your car and now your boat! Mom, can you forgive me?" Tears streamed down her cheeks.

I watched as blood trickled from a gash above her mouth. Cindy's tongue reached out to lick her swollen lip. She repeated urgently, "Mom, please forgive me!"

Almost as if I were watching the scene from a distance, I looked at the agonized plea etched on Cindy's face. Inwardly, I applied her plea for forgiveness not only to the damaged car and boat, but to her rebellious spirit which had caused me pain for years.

She was asking a lot. My unhappiness toward her rebellion had raised a barrier I had found hard to surmount; yet I knew God wanted me to forgive her, not only for today, but for all her past actions.

Finally, I answered. "Yes, Cindy, I forgive you—for everything." I felt God had already forgiven her; I only needed to confirm it. "I'm thankful you're alive and not badly hurt." The compassion and forgiving love I felt for my daughter was greater than it had ever been.

Later, sitting in the ambulance with sirens screaming, I experienced a deep contentment and peace. *Was I content because Cindy had asked my forgiveness, or because she had expressed sorrow for my pain and the wreckage of the boat?* No, there was a more personal reason.

Before I could speak to Cindy, a scene flashed through my mind. I was kneeling beside my bed, crying out for God's forgiveness. My face, like Cindy's now, was wet with tears, and my grief was real. "Lord, I'm sorry for the things I've done to grieve You," I cried.

In those moments, I had experienced the love and complete forgiveness of my Lord Jesus Christ. If my heavenly Father could so graciously forgive me, I could surely show forgiveness to my child.

In the hospital, Cindy and I were thoroughly examined and X-rays were taken. The doctor reported: "Despite the swelling, neither of you have broken bones. You were both mighty fortunate." My arm was put in a sling and Cindy's gash above her lip was sutured.

When the doctor left the room, Cindy turned and hugged me. "Oh, Mom, I'm so glad you're okay."

I hadn't realized how my unforgiving attitude toward Cindy had affected our relationship. Once my attitude became one of loving her just as she is, she was able to respond with love. Today our relationship is one of mutual love and understanding. Our boat was damaged beyond repair. But for both Cindy and me, the accident marked a new beginning.

Bear with each other and forgive whatever grievances you may have against one another. Forgive as the Lord forgave you. And over all these virtues put on love, which binds them all together in perfect unity (Colossians 3:13-14).

*This article first appeared in *Power for Living*, October 27, 1989, and was reprinted in the *Pentecostal Evangel*, May 12, 1991. Reprinted in *The Lookout*, July 22, 1990. Reprinted in *Live*, May 10, 1992. Reprinted in *The Wesleyan Woman*, Spring, 1994. This article was published in a shorter format in July, 1996, in *Journey*.

David, Julie, Gwen & Kerry
This, too, was an "Unforgettable Wedding," 1984.

13

Answered Prayers

... We have confidence before God and receive from him anything we ask, because we obey his commands and do what pleases him (1 John 3:21-22).

Give God Thanks in All Circumstances

God Meant It for Good

The Bread of Life Made Me Well

How Prayer Transformed My Marriage

God Provides Helpers

A Call to Pray

When Believers Pray, Miracles Happen

I cried out to him with my mouth; his praise was on my tongue. If I had cherished sin in my heart, the Lord would not have listened (Psalm 66:17-18).

❀ Give God Thanks in All Circumstances

My first husband and I were devastated when our daughter, Cindy, moved in with her husband-to-be before they were married. I'd always said it would kill me if one of my daughters lived with a man before marriage. My husband, Harold, ordered me not to step inside of their home because of the disgrace he felt and to show Cindy how she'd grieved him. It made me think how my heavenly Father must grieve when I don't follow His will.

A number of years later I found myself contemplating a divorce. Divorce was the last offense against God I'd ever felt I'd be guilty of as a Christian. However, I couldn't live with a man who blasphemed the name of my Lord. I never made a harder decision.

It was only later I could give thanks to God and that was after I'd married Kerry. I thanked God for a husband who loved to pray with me. For years I had been praying for my husband to pray with me. Kerry was the husband God had picked to pray with me mornings, evenings, during difficult times, and whenever the Spirit moved us to pray.

It was amazing to me that my prayers were answered through something as repugnant as divorce.

That was when I saw it is necessary to give God thanks in all circumstances. He has the power to make even the bad things in our life work for good if we love Him.

Be joyful always; pray continually; give thanks in all circumstances, for this is God's will for you in Christ Jesus (1 Thessalonians 5:16-18).

❀ God Meant It for Good

Through our divorce, positive things happened to both Harold and me.

What had once been a thriving marriage had become a suffocating life where at times both of us could barely breathe. The enthusiastic, artistic, and creative person I once had been had nearly vanished from sight.

Breaking free from an unhealthy marriage helped both of us to grow and our mates found God. This is how God can make a bad situation work for good.

Harold married a wonderful Japanese woman who loves him very much, and now he has a dog for a pet. When he was married to me he didn't want pets, but Keko had a dog who loved Harold and it's hard not to love a pet who adores you.

Harold found a new way to express himself by cooking. Now he loves to cook. When married to me he didn't know how to boil water because I did all the cooking.

Because Terry told Keko how their father had loved working in the church, she joined a nearby Lutheran church and came to know the Lord.

God sent Kerry that night we joined Parents without Partners, to befriend me and help me over rough times. He also knew I would witness to Kerry about my faith and that he would receive Jesus as his Lord and Savior. In time he knew we would marry.

Harold had already married Keko before Kerry and I became engaged, and Kerry's first wife had also been married for a number of years, so in the eyes of the church we attended, Kerry and I were free to marry.

Because of our divorce, Kerry and Keko came to know the Lord. It's absolutely amazing how God took something as ugly as divorce and worked it all for good.

Harold had some tragic illnesses several years after he married Keko. He became so ill his bodily functions were shutting down. The doctors said he would be gone within days and Cindy and Terry were called to his bedside.

When I heard how sick Harold was my heart grieved. The thing that alarmed me most was my fear that he was still completely out of fellowship with God. I prayed with all my heart that he would live until he had become reconciled to his Lord and Savior, Jesus Christ.

I told Terry that I had prayed for her father to live and she responded by saying, "It's too late, Mom. His kidneys have shut down and all his vital signs are turning off. Prayer is not going to help him now."

But that didn't stop me because I knew that all things are possible with God, and I continued to pray that he would turn back to the Lord before he died.

Harold did pass away in 1999, twelve years after my prayer. Terry told me Keko's minister visited with him before he died. I pray I will see both Keko and Harold in heaven.

And the prayer offered in faith will make the sick person well; the Lord will raise him up. If he has sinned he will be forgiven (James 5:15).

Gwen Lawan Johnson

🏵 The Bread of Life Made Me Well

Eating food made me sick! My blood pressure soared to dangerous heights. It became so high I was susceptible to a heart attack or a stroke. Medications were not helping. The systolic blood pressure reached nearly two hundred and the lower diastolic pressure went as high as one hundred and forty, but stayed around one twenty-six.

After food testing, I was diagnosed as a "universal food reactor," which meant I reacted in a hypersensitive manner to every food I ate. The constant stress of certain chemicals, pollens, and molds in my environment to which I was also allergic had weakened my immune system. I suffered blinding headaches, severe muscle spasms, and even memory loss and confusion after eating. My weight had dropped to 103 pounds and I am five feet nine!

Even the injections to build my tolerance to molds and pollens had to be stopped.

"I can't give you any more injections," Daniel Summerfield, M.D., told me. "We can't take the risk. Your immune system is far too brittle," he explained.

Just when I thought I'd finally found a way to feel better I was told this bad news. Dr. Summerfield had been sure that small injections of the molds and pollens that bothered me, would build my immunity to odors in my environment so foods wouldn't bother me so much. However, after every shot I would get something that acted like the flu. My head would be all stopped up, my throat hurt and was inflamed and I ached all over. It was true the injections hadn't helped but had made my intolerance to foods worse.

Now the doctor said the injections to build my tolerance to molds and pollens had to be stopped. "You have two choices: The first is to enter a completely sterile environment in a special hospital in Texas. However, when you return to your normal environment you could become even worse," the doctor warned. "Or you can rotate the foods you eat so that no one food is eaten more often than every five days. We'll make you a diet from the foods to which you showed the least reaction." By waiting for five days, I would build up an acute reaction to those foods to which I was intolerant, so I would know to drop the trigger food from my diet.

For other foods I would not be exposing myself often enough to build an overload reaction.

I left the doctor's office extremely upset, clutching the diet they had made from foods that I reacted to the least. I walked around in a daze trying to comprehend everything the doctor had just told me. I certainly didn't want to enter a sterile place if I might be worse after I came out. I knew at times they put people in a bubble who reacted to so many things in the environment. God created me, so I knew He had a reason for allowing me to strike out again when it came to injections making me well.

After about ten minutes I returned to my car, opened the door and slid in. I bowed my head and prayed, "Lord, only You can help me now. If I could just stop eating and breathing I'd have it made."

When the reality of what I had just prayed hit me, I had to laugh, even though it summed up the hopelessness of my situation. I had finally admitted only God alone could help me.

On the way home, I talked to my Lord as I often do when I'm driving:

"Lord, I know You are trying to tell me something. You've proved to me I can't run my own life. I'm sick and I'm miserable. I give up. I'm ready to try it Your way. I'm giving You complete control of my life. You certainly will do a better job than I've done. I know you have the power to heal me, so if eating one food at a time on a rotation diet is the way You want to heal me, I'm willing to eat that way, but I need Your help all the way."

I had so many food intolerances, it was hard to find enough foods to keep making up diets. My health got worse before it got better. The first month of eating one food at a time seemed impossible. However, with encouragement from Kerry and by exercising my faith in the Lord, I continued. Many times I wanted to give up but my husband kept reminding me that my one-sided headaches were coming less often. The swelling in my joints had diminished and the severe muscle spasms were less frequent. I still had problems with memory and an irritable bowel. Once I learned to leave out all the foods that contained bakers' and brewers yeast, anything containing processed sugar and flour, I became better. Six years later I learned about the yeast, candida albicans, and how staying on antibiotics for more than two months while I had pneumonia, probably elevated the growth of the Candida in my digestive system and caused me to become intolerant to so many foods. The yeast building up in my digestive system, plus the injections to stop my intolerance to pollens and molds had furthered my outrageous reactions including serious memory problems. Foods containing sugar made the candida grow and had to be avoided. Years later my doctor at Kaiser gave me nystatin to get rid of the candida yeast in my digestive tract. That helped tremendously.

Leaving yeast and flour out of my diet meant no bread. However, I learned from the Word that Jesus is the Bread of Life. Jesus said,

"... I am the bread of life. He who comes to me will never go hungry, and he who believes in me will never be thirsty" (John 6:35).

"I have food to eat you know nothing about.... My food... is to do the will of him who sent me and to finish his work" (John 4:32,34).

I, too, wanted to do my Father's will. I prayed that Jesus would come live in me, and show me how to live life His way, so I would do my heavenly Father's will.

God has taught me many things during the past twenty years, but the most important thing was that Jesus needed to be present living in me, before I could make Him Lord over my life. During this difficult period I also learned that I can trust God completely in all situations. I found that by thanking God in all things, good or bad, I had a great peace and a joy I hadn't known before. Also, each time I chose to do God's will rather than my own, I experienced a peace and joy that was beyond my human understanding.

God cleansed my inner being by restoring my spirit with His Holy Spirit. He taught me to focus on Him and His will for my life. He gave me the strength to deal with my wounded emotions, and filled me with His tender love. However, before I could be healed emotionally, I needed to be cleansed of hurts deep within my being.

Being born in the midst of the Depression, I'd heard my mother often say, "The last thing we needed right then was another baby." As I grew, I often recalled this and other hurtful remarks she had made about me. Jesus made me see I needed to forgive my mother totally and stop feeling sorry for myself. In addition to releasing these sins to Jesus, (He'd already paid for them on the cross), there were my sins of worry and complaining.

I'd done what many people do. I'd tried to add Jesus to my old life instead of allowing Him to fill a clean vessel emptied of injurious habits and sins.

Once I made Him Lord of my life, He began to empty me of all my destructive habits, which had kept me from enjoying a full life in Him. Up until the time I'd given God control, I'd tried to worry things into happening the way I wanted them to turn out. Often my prayers had just been begging God to give me my own way. I continually struggled to do things in my own strength. Using my strength, I failed. Only when Jesus gave me His strength was I able to overcome the negative attitudes and the wounded emotions that kept me from being an effective Christian. I also needed God's strength to stay on my strict diet.

I still have to rotate foods. For breakfast, I usually have only one fruit and once a week I can eat rice and then I skip about four days and have rye flakes. I have a salad or soup for lunch but not the same vegetables two days in a row. In the evening I allow myself meat, one vegetable, and a starch.

I believe the discipline of eating this way has been good for me, and it has taught me self-control, which is one of the fruits of the Spirit. I generally write before I eat, because after I eat, foods still tend to dull my thinking and sometimes I find I've been writing the same thing over and over. Kerry calls it, "thinking like a sausage."

I wrote a manuscript about my search for health. Although it has not been published, it has been read by several people who I met, who endured the same types of blinding headaches, ear infections, sinusitis, arthritis, and weird pains all over their body, and muscle spasms. They read my manuscript and followed my suggestions and they came out of the pain just as I did. I'm sorry more doctors don't understand what foods can do in causing illness. At least, once a person knows it is foods that are keeping them sick, they can recognize there is hope. My prayer to be well was answered, but it takes faith and refusing to eat all those things I'd like to eat. I'm restricted, but if I maintain this diet I feel better than I ever did in my life before, and I know when I have to stop eating a food when I get one of my bad reactions. Many foods I can eat again if I wait six months or more. For the first time chocolate started giving me almost instant migraines, so I'm off of it at present along with wheat, corn, yeast, grapes, and lemons.

But the best thing of all that came about because of my chronic illnesses is the new relationship between the Lord and me. Even as Christ was raised from the dead, never to die again, so I have been resurrected to new life in

Christ Jesus. I look forward to each new day wondering what new and exciting thing God has in store for me.

Therefore, if anyone is in Christ, he is a new creation; the old has gone, the new has come! (2 Corinthians 5:17).

*This article was published as "The Food of Life Made Me Well," in the July/August edition of *Faith at Work.*

✿ How Prayer Transformed My Marriage

Wives often expect husbands to change without changing themselves. I know, because early in our marriage I was one of those wives.

The Lord blessed me with a handsome, distinguished looking husband who radiated warmth and compassion. All my friends thought Kerry was charming. I soon found out, however, that Kerry didn't want to be told what to do. To him every suggestion I made sounded as if I was ordering him around. One of us would have to change!

Then one Sunday in Bible class, our pastor made a statement that awakened my spiritual awareness. He said, "Jesus lived the only life acceptable to God." If Jesus' life was the only life acceptable to God, I reasoned, it was His life I needed. After that thought echoed through my mind time after time I prayed, "Lord, I love Kerry. I want to be the best wife possible. I want to love him with an unselfish love, the way You love me when I'm not very lovable. Please, let Jesus live His life in me, guiding me to His perfect love."

God's answer to this prayer transformed my marriage. Of course, we had to grow into the changes, but slowly they came. Before the prayer, when I gave love, I expected a certain kind of response. If I didn't receive that reaction, I'd feel hurt and rejected. After the prayer, I no longer required a response. The joy of loving Kerry became sufficient in itself. This is what God wanted us to have for each other: love that is given without calculation of cost, gain to the giver, or merit on the part of the receiver.

Another thing I learned was to replace selfish reactions. Kerry came home and told me, "My company is giving me the chance to go to Chicago for a month's schooling which would help me in my job, but I'd have to be away for a whole month."

You can't go away and leave me that long, was my first thought. Immediately, an inner sensitivity made me aware of my selfishness, so the answer

I gave was, "Kerry, I'll really miss you, but it does sound like a wonderful opportunity. If it will help you in your work, do it." He later received a promotion and a raise.

Another problem I had was making assumptions, like planning for the week-end without consulting Kerry first. All week long I'd think how great the new wallpaper I'd bought would look in our bathroom, expecting Kerry to hang the paper. Sometimes I'd look forward to taking a drive to the beach. When Saturday finally arrived, I'd finish making the bed and run downstairs to spring my idea on Kerry. If I found him in the garage working on one of the cars, I'd feel angry. "I suppose you're planning to work on that truck all day!" I'd say in an accusing way.

Jesus showed me that I was jealous of my husband's time, and the cars that were taking him away from me. I learned to discuss my plans for the weekend with Kerry ahead of time. If he told me, "Honey, I really need to work on the truck," I felt grateful he provided us with safe and reliable transportation.

Another thing I had to learn was adapting to inconveniences. Most evenings, I'd have dinner ready by 6:00 p.m. In the past when Kerry called at 5:55 p.m. to let me know he'd be late, I'd scold, "Do you mean you haven't left work yet?"

After my prayer, I would calmly thank Kerry for calling to let me know he would be late. Then, he'd say, "Gwen, I really appreciate your being so patient with me. I know I should have called earlier." This caused Kerry to be patient with me.

I found that Kerry and my praying together enhanced intimacy. Kerry was a wonderful prayer partner. When we became united in prayer with God, we experienced a spiritual oneness that enriched not only our relationship with Christ, but with each other. We marveled how through prayer, God took seemingly impossible situations in our lives, and the lives of those we loved, and turned them into blessings. No situation was too difficult. We learned to thank and praise God in every circumstance, good or bad, knowing He would work it for good if we loved and trusted Him.

The image of God reflected in the one I loved, brought joy and fulfillment to our marriage. When both of us reflected God's image, there was a beautiful harmony of body and spirit. Even our sexual relationship had a new dimension. United in Christ, the spirituality of sex came to transcend the beauty of our physical oneness. There might be times, however, when Kerry was too tired or too sick to be the romantic lover I conjured up in romantic daydreams. During times like these, I saved myself and Kerry needless worry and future failure, by appreciating the hugs and kisses I did get and by assuring my mate, "For tonight, I just want to be held close in your arms."

Sharing Christ's love was our goal. By ourselves, we are unable to establish this type of relationship. I tried to add Christ to my "self" life, but I never achieved the love, peace, and joy the Bible promises. Doing Christ's will had to become more important to me than having my own way. Kerry's reactions were a response to Christ's unselfish love at work in me and our being united with Christian prayer.

Kerry's reaction to a "higher love" showed in the affectionate way he looked at me when he reached for my hand or his arm encircled my waist; the thoughtful things he did for me; the kiss that brushed my cheek or landed gently on my neck; the loving way he accepted my peculiarities and loved me in spite of them. A day rarely passed without Kerry telling me, "I thank God for you."

When I occasionally reverted back to old habits, it was a shock to both of us. First, I became aware that I was not being motivated by Christ's love. I stopped right then and thanked God for showing me I was in the wrong. My being aware that I had reverted to my old self-centered attitude, proved to both of us how much better our marriage was when we practiced Jesus' love, rather than our own self-centered ways. Secondly, I'd confess the sin placing me out of God's will, and ask for His power to overcome that sin.

Third, I asked for God's forgiveness, and then I'd ask Kerry to forgive me.

Finally, I'd tell Kerry how thankful I was that he was my mate and how happy I was that God loves and forgives sinners. Then we would have a discussion on what had just happened, which was followed by hugs and kisses. How simply a relationship can be restored when the problem is dealt with immediately! I believe many marriages can be transformed if God, through Christ, is given first place in the marriage.

"If you love me, you will obey what I command. And I will ask my Father, and he will give you another counselor to be with you forever— the Spirit of truth (John 14:15-16).

*This article was previously published in *Christian Living*, August, 1990. It was reprinted in *Live*, January 1992.

🌸 God Provides Helpers

One morning a charming looking woman walked up to me at church and said, "You look like a friendly person. I'm here alone. May I sit with you?"

"Why I'd be delighted!" I introduced myself and learned this lovely woman's name was Martha. "My husband is ushering and it will feel much better to have someone to sit with," I told Martha.

Church hadn't started yet, so we had a few moments to chat.

Martha stated that she'd heard our pastor speaking on the radio that morning. "I decided to come over here, rather than attending my church. You know there is something I've really been missing at my church. I used to help a woman with Backyard Bible Clubs, but her husband was transferred to Oregon and I just can't tell you how much I miss working with children."

I looked at her beaming. "You don't have to miss children any longer because I have Backyard Bible Clubs every summer, and on Easter and Christmas vacations when I can get a group of kids together. What I really need is someone to teach the songs. For years Kathy helped me out, but her husband's company recently transferred him to North Carolina. That's why God sent you to talk to me. You had a need to help and I have a need for a helper."

"I can certainly help. I sing in the choir and I already know many of the songs."

I was thrilled. "God sent you here today and He's the One who directed you to me. You're an answer to prayer."

The kids love Martha and she's been a wonderful addition to my staff.

While talking to a Sunday School teacher, I told her I wanted to hold a class in August, this year. "I'll be happy to come help you with crafts, and if you want to do a puppet show after your lesson to see what the kids learned, I can do that too," she volunteered.

Isn't it marvelous that God takes time to see that I have a staff to help me with my Backyard Bible Club? And the staff He provides couldn't be better.

Because of the Lord's great love His compassions never fail. They are new every morning; great is your faithfulness (Lamentations 3:22-23).

❀ A Call to Pray

"I need your prayers," Bill Fitzsimmons announced when he attended our fellowship meeting for the first time. "Both of my kidneys are failing and I need a kidney transplant."

In 1971 doctors had warned Bill his kidneys would fail in fifteen to twenty years. The time had come. More than twenty years had passed since Bill had been diagnosed with Berger's disease, which eventually brings about kidney failure.

"Pray for a kidney that will work well in my body. Not only does the donated kidney have to match my blood type, it also needs ten additional characteristics to make it compatible for a successful transplant," Bill told us.

"Some patients receive kidneys from immediate family members, while others, like me, have to wait for a new kidney to be donated by a person who has passed on," Bill explained.

I left our fellowship meeting that night knowing I'd made the right decision when I decided to leave my kidneys to be used by someone like Bill. I could see how Bill's getting a kidney could become a matter of life and death. Until a compatible kidney was found he would have to depend on hemodialysis. Without the kidney machine Bill would die.

Minor surgery had enlarged a vein in Bill's arm so two needles could be inserted. Blood from the vein was pumped through a plastic tube to the dialysis machine, which removed the waste products and fluids from Bill's blood and to an adjacent vein. Processing the blood through the machine for four to six hours, three or four times a week was enough to control the level of waste products in Bill's blood.

After Bill asked for prayer, Kerry and I prayed that night that God would give Bill the strength to continue working and that a compatible kidney would be found.

A curious and wonderful occurrence took place in my life. God put on me a great urgency to pray for Bill. I'd awake in the middle of the night, knowing I must pray. I prayed while I drove the car, ironed, shopped for groceries, any time of the day or night when God urged me to pray for the right kidney for Bill. I couldn't even remember praying this much for a family member. The need became etched in my mind.

Because of the urging from God, I knew this prayer was in His will and that He would surely supply Bill with a kidney. I just didn't know God's timetable.

Bill's attitude was one of expectation, but he was willing to go along with God's program, in God's timing. Some people insist God heal them instantly or in a certain way, but Bill left this matter up to God's will. From my experience, that pleases God. God's Spirit continued to challenge me to pray consistently and in a dedicated manner. I felt happy to know how much God cares about those He loves and I was excited that He called me to pray.

At our April meeting, Bill had announced his need for a kidney. By the July meeting, Bill had an announcement to make. "They've found a kidney for me. It's a miracle for me to receive a kidney this quickly."

We praised and thanked God. In my heart I knew my continuous prayer had made a difference. I was filled with the knowledge of our need to obey God when He urges us to pray for someone. Now Bill asked that we pray that the new kidney would work well in his body and that his body would not reject the new transplant.

Unfortunately, the body's immune system treats any transplanted organ as if it were an infecting organism and tries to destroy the new transplant by the action of the white cells and the antibodies.

Bill's surgery took place a few days later and I prayed before, during and after the surgery that all would go well. God had me continue in prayer until the kidney was working well and Bill was praising God for giving him a second chance with a new kidney. Fortunately, the new kidney could do the work of two.

Bill attended the August meeting to thank all of us who had been praying. "I've been blessed. I was never in a great deal of pain. When my kidneys began to fail I grew weaker and anemic, but was still able to work. I live each day knowing it is by God's grace and the prayers of my friends that I'm still here," he told us.

Our prayers had worked. Now it was time to thank and praise God for His remarkable healing power working in Bill's favor.

There are many things we can pray for regularly, such as God's strength for our lives, His love, His healing power, and His wisdom; they are all available through prayer. However, God's Holy Spirit may direct us to pray for certain individuals. The impulse that leads us to pray is God's voice within us. We can rejoice when His voice compels us to pray, and we must not reject such urging. These prayers bring joy to our heart when God answers them. We become His servants to bring about His will in the world.

All prayers may not be answered as quickly as this one, but continue to pray with the faith to believe it is God's will. Be still, listening for His urging to pray and follow that urging. I have never failed to have a prayer answered when I pray at God's urging.

"Therefore I tell you, whatever you ask for in prayer, believe that you have received it, and it will be yours" (Mark 11:24).

❀ When Believers Pray, Miracles Happen

Dan Lagasse was born with cystic fibrosis but that didn't keep him from being a missionary. He and his wife, DeAnna, learned the Kurdish language and were sent by our congregation to witness to the Kurds in Germany.

Dan served gladly, but there came a time when he could no longer breathe without oxygen. Later, came a serious time he could barely breathe even with oxygen, and he returned to the United States. The only hope remaining to keep him alive was a pair of new lungs.

When I heard about this, God prompted me to pray while I washed, while in the car driving, while I worked in the garden, and no matter where I was, God put it on my heart to pray for Dan. During the night I was awakened, and knew I was to pray that the right lungs would be available for Dan that would work in his body. I knew Dan would get the lungs, because God was putting it on my heart to pray like I'd never prayed for anyone before. God would not have me pray if it was not His will. Many others including his family prayed as well.

We got excited when we heard there was a set of lungs available, but they were bruised and Dan's doctor was not interested in damaged lungs for Dan. Our prayers resumed.

Dan's hospitalization insurance only had a few more weeks before it would be canceled. He had nearly depleted the maximum amount of the policy. Just when he was down to the wire on his insurance coverage, he was offered two lungs and a heart. They planned to give his heart to another person who needed a heart transplant.

His spectacular surgery was performed at Stanford Medical Hospital in Palo Alto, California.

After eleven and one half hours in surgery and thirteen surgical procedures including a sternotomy, and thoracotomy, he had lost thirty-two units of blood. Blood was spurting out everywhere. Doctors couldn't stop the bleeding and the chaplain had been called. The operating doctor said, "There is nothing further I can do to stop the bleeding. I am sorry." Then he sent for the hospital chaplain to comfort Dan's wife in her grief.

Dan's wife, DeAnna, and other members of his family and congregation, kneeled in the hospital room to pray, and I was home praying through all this time waiting for the news that the operation had been a success.

While all of us prayed fervently for the bleeding to stop, it stopped quite suddenly.

"Today I have witnessed a miracle!" the operating physician exclaimed.

For the next thirty-one days, Dan lay in one position in ICU, connected to a respirator. He could not talk, eat or drink, turn his head or his body.

"God gave me peace," he later told me. The doctor said he wished they could bottle Dan's peace for other patients. A tube went down his throat into his lungs, one-half inch around and eight inches long. He developed complications; his head started swelling. It grew as large as a basketball. His eyelids hung down over his cheeks and his lips drooped down over his chin. The Doctor took pictures of this strange sight. Dan said, "I looked like something out of a comic book, only worse." The doctors couldn't find why the blood was all rushing to his head.

Finally the problem was located. A blood clot was blocking the superior vena cava vein, which carries the blood from the upper body to the heart. When the vena cava was blocked by a blood clot, the blood bypassed the heart and went to Dan's head rather than to his heart. They didn't dare give him a blood thinner or he'd bleed to death. They located a doctor who had a machine that could suction the clot from inside the heart. The Doctor suctioned out blood twice. Then the fluid began to build up inside of Dan's tissues. Every time someone touched his skin, water would drip out. The weight of the fluid was so heavy in his arms he couldn't move them. After giving him lasix to remove the water, he passed twenty-five pounds or three gallons of urine in one night.

In order to prevent his body from rejecting the new lungs and heart, the doctors administered one thousand milligrams of prednisone along with other drugs to help his body accept the new organs. Dan became psychotic. When one of the other ministers from church came to visit him, he told him the nurse was trying to poison him by putting frozen yogurt in the feeding tube to his veins. He said he really believed that what he was saying was true.

The donor whose heart and lungs he received had a virus and the virus had gotten into the tissue of the heart and lungs. It took five weeks of antibiotics to get over the viral infection.

We got the word that many things were happening to Dan. His body fought the new organs, containing a virus that the original owner had at death, and Dan was fighting for that virus to be healed as well as praying to be cured. At times it looked as if it was hopeless, but Dan's wife had been assured by the Lord that Dan would live to see their two young daughters one day get married. She held on to her faith. At home I didn't know Dan was suffering from so many things, but I knew he was not out of danger yet. After the operation I was praying his body would not reject the organs.

I was in almost continual prayer for this godly young man. I'd gotten acquainted with Dan at the Exchanged Life seminar when we were asked to interview each other. During the interview I'd come to admire and have great respect for him and his family.

This operation took place more than four years ago and Dan's daughters now have trouble keeping up with him—even at Disneyland! When believers pray, marvelous things happen. This is just one miracle that happened as a result of people with faith praying persistently for a missionary whom we all loved. We wanted him to enjoy life with normal lungs, and we all were able to see him breathe easily like other people. What a wonderful God we serve!

Dan is pastor of Global Outreach for Los Gatos Christian Church, Los Gatos, California.

Be devoted to one another in brotherly love. Honor one another above yourselves.... Be joyful in hope, patient in affliction, faithful in prayer (Romans 12:10,12).

14
The Joy of Giving

"Give, and it will be given to you. A good measure, pressed down, shaken together and running over, will be poured into your lap. For with the measure you use, it will be measured to you" (Luke 6:38).

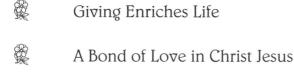 Giving Enriches Life

 A Bond of Love in Christ Jesus

 A Surprise for Mother's Day

 Keep Giving the Gospel Message

An Easter to Remember

"Will a man rob God? Yet you rob me. But you ask, 'How do we rob you?' In tithes and offerings.... Bring the whole tithe into the storehouse, that there may be food in my house. Test me in this," says the Lord Almighty, "and see if I will not throw open the flood-gates of heaven and pour out so much blessing that you will not have room enough for it.... Then all the nations will call you blessed, for yours will be a delightful land," say the Lord Almighty (Malachi 3:8,10,12).

❀ Giving Enriches Life

I started tithing when I was ten. Although my mother never talked about tithing, I saw her drop our last dollar bill in the collection plate at church. That afternoon someone brought a goat to breed, and mother received five dollars.

"See," my mother said, holding up a five dollar bill. "I gave our last dollar and it has returned five fold." I never forgot that day.

When Pastor Jesse explained tithing meant giving one cent out of every dime, I said to myself, *I can do that.* Immediately I started tithing out of my allowance and from money I made selling vegetables from the garden.

Later when I worked at J.C. Penney's in San Francisco, I had the pleasure of meeting Mr. Penney in person. He started his empire by paying cash for everything he bought and by giving a tithe to the Lord.

However, if a person tithes because he wants more money, it will not work. I knew a man who decided to tithe and he got so much work that he'd made the extra amount for the tithe during the first three months that year. He said, "Boy! That tithing business really works." He pledged three times the amount he'd pledged the year before, thinking he'd make three times more than the year before. However, he learned that trying to make money from tithing doesn't work. What works is trusting God's promises.

On our last trip to Washington state and Canada, on a ferry home from Victoria Island, I found myself sitting across from two young people who looked like teenagers. Somehow we started up a conversation and I told them about our wonderful trips in the R.V. going around the United States, and the fantastic cruises we'd taken all around the world. The young man told me his grandfather, who was a minister, had taken him on a cruise and how much fun he'd had. "I hope we'll be taking cruises like you and your husband have someday." Then I learned these two young people weren't teenagers but a couple in their twenties on their honeymoon.

I told them I believed the reason we'd been so bountifully blessed was that we took God's challenge to tithe ten percent of our income for the Lord's work in the world. Then I told them about the passage in Malachi 3:10 where God issues a challenge, saying, *"Test me in this,"* [about giving a whole tithe] *says the Lord Almighty, "and see if I will not throw open the floodgates of heaven and pour out so much blessing that you will not have room enough for it."*

The young people seemed interested in my belief that I had God to thank for the trips we'd taken. I told them the blessing didn't start right away, but after faithfully giving even more than a tithe, I had booked a cruise to Italy, and sure enough when the time came, I'd been able to save up the money for that cruise. We loved that trip and we wanted to see more of God's wonderful world. Every time we booked a cruise about one year ahead, the money was available when we needed it. "Sometimes it did mean denying ourselves something to give to God first," I told the couple.

"Do you feel the money has to go only to the church?" the young man asked.

"No. God's work is feeding the poor and starving people of the world, and seeing that the gospel is preached to every people by helping support missions. Bibles need to be sent or taken to the prisons, and to countries who haven't heard the good news about God's Word."

"What about money to help send doctors to those who need medical aid?" the pretty blonde girl asked.

"Certainly that, too, is doing God's work in the world." We had a good discussion about what sorts of organizations would be considered in the tithe.

We reached our destination and I bid these two delightful young people goodbye.

I looked up and saw the young man coming back. "Did you forget something?" I asked.

"I wanted to thank you for sharing how God has enriched your life through giving. I wanted to let you know that we are going to start tithing. We hope God will bless us as He has you."

"Oh, He will because His promises are true. If you start doing this in the beginning of your marriage, it will get you started off right. One day you'll be extremely happy you made this decision."

I was astounded. I had no idea that my testimony had touched them that much. I do believe if we take God's promises as true, that they will come true in our lives.

Pastor Jesse never knew what an influence he had in my tithing, and I never told my mother how her example influenced me, too. I have to admit there were times early in my first marriage, when my daughter, Terry, was little that I probably missed giving a tithe, because she was so difficult in church and they didn't have a nursery; I was so worn out, I quit going to church while she was small and I didn't tithe.

There were times when I told my husband, "That's too much to give," when he wanted to give a large sum to start the Bethel Series in our church. I didn't think we could afford it. We never missed that money.

Now I ask myself, "How can I give more?"

Since we have four bedrooms, I have taken a boarder and all the money he pays for staying nights here, I give over and above my tithe, because there are charities that I want to help support besides the tithe I give to church.

What changed my attitude? I believe it is God's Holy Spirit working in me who shows me those missionaries and organizations who need extra money. Besides, I have enjoyed the bountiful blessings of God, and I truly want others to experience the joy of giving.

No one will ever convince me that it is impossible to tithe. It is not only possible it is necessary. Once a person starts giving out of their love for God it makes one feel blessed to be charitable. God loves a cheerful giver. Remember giving is not only in the form of money, it is also using our time and talents to help others.

Giving even more than a tithe becomes easy. Keep in mind that it is impossible to outgive God.

We must help the weak, remembering the words the Lord Jesus himself said: "It is more blessed to give than to receive" (Acts 20:35b).

❀ A Bond of Love in Christ Jesus

Although my husband, Kerry, and I had not previously considered a cruise to Italy, when I read the especially low price for the two-week trip, I told our travel agent, "Book us!"

Afterward, I felt concerned. *Was this the proper way to spend our money?*

I wondered if I could be of service on a cruise ship. While seeking what God would have us do I remained silent. Before long I knew there would be something my husband and I could do. God would show me when the time came. While packing, I slipped some song sheets, and a New Life Study Testament into our carry-on luggage.

The plane we were to transfer to in Dallas, Texas was grounded. Its replacement arrived in Texas over an hour after our ship had been scheduled to sail out of Florida, headed for Italy. Representatives for the cruise ship met our plane in Florida and drove us to the waiting ship. When other passengers learned we were from California, they teased us, "Oh, you're the reason we sailed three hours late."

I smiled, "I knew you wouldn't leave without us."

We were exhausted from our twelve-hour trip, but we enjoyed a late dinner and the evening entertainment. We returned to our room at almost midnight. The Sunday schedule had been slipped under our door. The only church service listed was a Catholic Mass. We attended the mass.

Later we talked to the Italian priest about having a Protestant Non-denominational service for the following Sunday. At first, Father Don stated there was no provision for any other religious service. He provided a short mass every day, and a service on Sunday, he explained. When we asked if we could conduct a Protestant service for the following week, Father Don agreed to meet with us a few days later to discuss it.

Father Don was young, probably in his late twenties. He rushed in late for our appointment, breathless, apologizing for his tardiness. A tousled piece of straight black hair fell across his forehead over his black horn-rimmed glasses. Words tumbled out when he spoke. His Italian accent was charming.

We explained to Father Don that we were prepared to help provide a Sunday service for the non-Catholic believers aboard ship. He appeared happy to have our help in planning the service. It seemed as if it were something he'd wanted to do, but hadn't quite known how to go about it.

We picked four well known hymns from those I'd packed, including "Amazing Grace." A piece of prose entitled, "We're Hungry, Lord," was printed on the top of that song sheet. I had never noticed it before, but I could see the words were perfect for a responsive reading. I inserted the words, **Reader** and **Response** in the appropriate places. Finally, my husband and I shook hands with Father Don. We were prepared for a Sunday service.

The Non-denominational service began at five o'clock on Sunday evening in the Tropicana Lounge. Father Don opened the service with a prayer. He welcomed everyone and read,

Rejoice in the Lord always. I will say it again: Rejoice!... The Lord is near. Do not be anxious about anything, but in everything, by prayer and petition, with thanksgiving, present your requests to God. And the peace of God, which transcends all understanding, will guard your hearts and your minds in Christ Jesus (Philippians 4:4-7).

He followed the reading with an interesting sermonette, saying, "God is indeed near. He is right here with us in the Tropicana Lounge."

When he finished his short sermon, he introduced Kerry who led us in singing "Amazing Grace."

Then it was my turn.

Walking to the microphone at the center of the stage, I shook so hard I wondered if I could do what we'd planned. The passage, *I can do everything through him who gives me strength* (Philippians 4:13) came to mind. Drawing on His strength I spoke to the nearly two hundred people gathered. "'We're hungry,' might sound a little strange for people on a cruise, but this reading is speaking of a different kind of hunger—our hunger for God." It was remarkable how this writing by an anonymous author delivered a perfect message for people who had all the food they could want on a cruise ship.

"We're hungry for Your kind of power, love, and joy. Feed us with Your rich food." With those words the responsive reading closed and I announced our next hymn, "Softly and Tenderly Jesus is Calling."

After the hymn my husband, Kerry, came to speak. "Just about a year ago I heard the dreaded word cancer come from my doctor's lips." Kerry told how he'd become anxious and fearful. One night he couldn't sleep and started to worry. He went downstairs and sat down at the kitchen table. The words hanging on a plaque on the wall caught his attention.

Do not be anxious about anything, but in everything, by prayer and petition, with thanksgiving, present your requests to God. And the peace of God, which transcends all understanding, will guard your hearts and your minds in Christ Jesus (Philippians 4:6-7).

"Immediately, I stopped and prayed," Kerry continued. "I knew it wasn't God's will for me to worry. If anxiety wasn't from God, then it had to be from Satan."

Every eye in the room was on Kerry, and a hush fell over the Tropicana Lounge.

"I did something I'd never done before. In the name of Jesus Christ, I requested the spirits of fear, worry, and anxiety to leave me alone. Then I thanked God, because the passage says to make our request with thanksgiving. After thanking God, I asked Him to use this cancer to work for good in my life and in the lives of others."

"An amazing thing happened," Kerry continued. "A marvelous peace spread throughout my body. It was difficult to believe I could experience such peace after being so scared. I've never had another anxious or fearful moment about cancer from that day to this."

I glanced where Father Don was seated and watched him take off his glasses to wipe his eyes.

"My wife, Gwen, and I went to Hawaii, and had a wonderfully relaxing time, free from worry, fear, and anxiety. A minister from Wales who spoke at my brother-in law's church, every evening that week said just the words I needed to hear. Dead or alive I knew I belonged to my Lord and Savior, Jesus Christ. I knew I could draw strength from Him."

By taking this trip, Kerry had time for his anemic blood to become normal and he was able to donate his own blood to be used if needed during the surgery. After surgery, they announced Kerry's growths were cancerous, but the doctors felt they had removed all of the cancer. My husband passed his tenth anniversary after the surgery without colon cancer reappearing.

After the last hymn, Father Don said a beautiful prayer and led all of us in the Lord's Prayer. The service closed with "Rock of Ages." We finished ten minutes before the Catholic Mass was to begin.

Two new friends we had met aboard the ship were Evelyn and her husband, Steve. They were Catholics, from New York and we had enjoyed their company throughout the trip. Evelyn had attended the Protestant service with us, and her husband, Steve, joined us later for the Catholic service. "I didn't know about Kerry's cancer. I'm glad I got to hear his testimony," Evelyn told me. While we were talking, I glimpsed a tender moment mirrored in her eyes. I turned just in time to see my husband, Kerry, and Father Don standing up on the stage embracing in Christian fellowship and love.

Later, Kerry described it as: "A moment in time when two men, a young Catholic priest and an older American Protestant, experienced a bond of fellowship in Christ Jesus."

The words from a song, "You will know they are Christians by their love, by their love," echoed in my brain.

"Thank You, Lord, that we are one in You," I whispered.

Kerry and I remained for Mass.

Father Don started by saying, "Sometimes we Catholics become so involved with one another, we forget to reach out to our other brothers and sisters in Christ. I have just witnessed a couple who aren't Catholic, who cared enough to reach out in love to their brothers and sisters, by preparing a Non-denominational service which we celebrated before this Mass. This same couple are worshipping here with us today to demonstrate their love for us and for our Lord and Savior, Jesus Christ."

What a moment of joy! Kerry and I had accomplished the work God intended.

"My command is this: Love each other as I have loved you" (John 15:12).

❀ A Surprise for Mother's Day

"Would you be a stand-in mother for Kerry and me this year on Mother's Day?" I inquired when I phoned my great-aunt Elsie who lived about sixty miles away. Aunt Elsie's only son, Dick, had passed away and my husband, Kerry, had lost his Mom a few months before. I knew from experience that the first Mother's Day after the loss of a mother is the most difficult, and I felt sure it would be hard on my Aunt without her son.

Aunt Elsie had broken her arm and then a few months later she'd fallen and broken her hip, so she'd be unable to go out to eat. I offered to prepare dinner and bring it along and eat it with her, since none of her relatives lived nearby.

She sounded very happy to have us coming to spend her first Mother's Day after her son's death. I decided to fix a leg of lamb with mashed potatoes and gravy, with a salad and asparagus. I also baked an apple pie. Lamb and apple pie were two of my aunt's favorites. She had no need for material things, but a plant always brightens a room, so I bought a beautiful large hydrangea plant loaded with blue blooms. When I stopped to pay for the plant, I noticed boxed orchids, and even though my common sense told me that my aunt couldn't go anywhere to wear it, a strong urge caused me to buy the orchid, too.

Aunt Elsie met us at the door. Kerry showed her the large blue hydrangea plant and she told him to put it on an end table in her living room. I presented the orchid corsage and pinned it on her dress. Aunt Elsie's eyes brimmed with tears.

"Dick always bought me an orchid for Mother's Day. When he died I thought I would never again receive another orchid," she told me.

"That's strange, because this is the first orchid I've ever bought for anyone," I admitted. "Do you suppose God led me to buy this orchid for you?"

"He must have prompted you to buy it because He knew how much it would mean to me," Aunt Elsie replied.

I gave my special aunt a big hug. My mother had died many years before, but once again I knew the joy of Mother's Day!

May he give you the desire of your heart and make all your plans succeed (Psalms 20:4).

❀ Keep Giving the Gospel Message

Looking back over her life, Julie recalls a day when she was a tiny toddler, and many people had gathered in her mother's bedroom. She'd tugged on her mother's sleeve, but her lifeless body did not respond. Later, when she grew older, she wondered if that was the day her mother had died in their home at Akiak, Alaska.

Growing up Julie could not understand why other kids had mamas and she didn't. She'd lived with her mother's sister and her grandmother, since her father made his living by fishing in the summer and hunting in the winter, taking him away from home for long periods of time. One day when Julie was about seven, her father was playing with her hair and he asked her, "How did you get these scars in your head?"

Julie was shocked. "I didn't know I had scars in my head." She thought quick and told her dad, "One day I fell and hit my head on a rock and another time I scraped it on a tree stump." Julie was too ashamed to tell him how her aunt hit her time and time again, so she made excuses for her injuries. She later recalled how she was beaten on the head until she fell to the ground unconscious.

One time her father came to pick her up at school. He found her clothes in tatters and her shoes had worn until her toes were exposed to the bitter cold of winter. Inquiring about his daughter he was told, "You'd better get her out of that home before that aunt of hers kills her." Even the people who told her father about the beatings, were not aware that Julie was not only battered and beaten, but sexually abused as well.

After living in her father's home for about a year, the next time he left to go fishing, he placed her in an orphanage run by a missionary. She didn't want to hear about God because she said religion was being forced on her. She ran away from the orphanage but they found her and brought her back. She got enough of the gospel message taught there that she never forgot it, although she couldn't understand a God who would allow a child to suffer the abuse she had.

In her teens, Julie started writing letters to boarding schools, hoping to leave the orphanage where she had to work hard, cleaning and caring for the younger children.

Finally, one school wrote they would accept her and she was transferred there, where she was one in a group of more than seven hundred children. While living at the boarding school, Julie was informed that her father had died.

She glared defiantly toward heaven, "There you go—picking on Julie again! Why out of more than seven hundred children did it have to be my father who died leaving me an orphan?" she asked.

Now Julie's hatred of God became etched into her very being as a part of her. She knew it wasn't right to hate God, so as she grew older, she suppressed her true feelings, only allowing the hatred to surface after she had a few drinks too many.

I met and talked with Julie at the health spa. My heart ached for her. Only because she had been drinking, was she able to confess her hatred toward God.

"Julie, the God you speak of is not the God I know. My God loves you." Each time I had the opportunity, I shared with her about the God who sent His Son Jesus, to die on the cross for our sins. I shared how good God had been to me, and how He loved her even though she hated Him. Her bitterness toward God appeared so deep, there seemed nothing any human could do or say to change her mind.

Unknown to me, Julie admitted herself into a recovery hospital and the day she was admitted she stopped drinking. It was June 23rd, 1980. She finally poured out her bitterness toward God and how much she hated Him for what He allowed her to suffer as a child. "You've been bottling this stuff up forty years, Julie. That's the most honest testimony we've ever heard. You'll feel better now for unloading your feelings," members of the hospital staff told her.

From the day she confessed her feelings, June 23rd, 1980 she never took another drink. After being discharged from the hospital she joined Alcoholics Anonymous. She disclosed her story to them and they gave her a twelve point program to work on. She did the first two steps but she couldn't make herself seek a higher power. For three years she was stuck on the third step. It seemed no one could encourage her to make peace with God.

She did come to see me and all the rest of her friends to whom she'd said hateful things during the time she was drinking, to ask forgiveness. But for nearly three years she stayed at the same point of recovery. Her friends forgave her but she could not forgive God for the things He allowed to happen to her as a child.

Quite unexpectedly, one Saturday evening, I glanced at the clock and told Kerry, "It's nearly eleven o'clock and too late to call Julie to invite her to go to church tomorrow."

Kerry looked startled. He knew I hadn't seen or talked to Julie for several years.

"Did she say she wanted to go?"

"No, but I think she might want to."

The next day I learned that Julie had looked at her clock at eleven and told a friend, "I wanted to call Gwen tonight to ask about going to church with her, but it's nearly eleven and too late to phone now."

I set the alarm clock early enough to call Julie the next morning, to give her time to dress for church, if she wanted to go. The next morning the alarm went off and I was reaching for my book of phone numbers when the phone rang. As I put the receiver to my ear I heard Julie's voice.

"What time are you two leaving for church this morning?" she asked. "I want to go with you."

"Julie I can't believe this! I was just getting ready to dial your number, to ask if you wanted to go with us." We hadn't seen each other for so long, she didn't even recognize me sitting in the car waiting for her, because much of my hair had turned white and I'd lost more than forty pounds. It was when I had problems eating food.

It may have been a long time since we'd seen each other, but that didn't keep me from knowing she wanted to attend church.

Later Julie said, "I think God put it in your mind to call me in case I chickened out about going to church."

When we arrived at church, I was disappointed that our senior minister was on vacation and that one of the younger ministers would be preaching. By divine appointment, the young minister preached the exact sermon Julie needed to hear. Later she would comment, "Every word he preached was for me!"

Near the end of the sermon, it was our minister's habit to invite any of those who wished guidance, counseling, or wanted to become members of our church to come forward to the counseling room. During the invitation time I bowed my head to pray. "Oh, God, let Your Holy Spirit move Julie out into the aisle and forward to the counseling room. She needs you so much. Please open her mind to Your will in her life." When I raised my head from praying, Julie was gone.

Inside the counseling room, through a flood of tears, Julie prayed to Jesus asking Him to forgive her for her hatred, and to come into her life in a real way, revealing Himself as her Lord and Savior. Before she asked Jesus into her life she said she was afraid to do anything or make any decisions. She lost that fear, and during the next week she bought herself a mobile home. She talked to her real estate agent and told her about receiving Jesus and becoming baptized. She said after doing that she lost her fear and was able to invest in a mobile home.

"I knew my real estate lady was a Christian, because when I told her, she gave me a big smile and squeezed my hand."

"I'm not alone anymore," Julie told me not long after she started attending church. "Jesus has entered my life as my Lord and my Savior from sin, and I've got all these brothers and sisters here at the church. I really know I belong in God's family of believers."

The peace and joy that came into Julie's life were beautiful to behold. The lines of bitterness vanished from her face and the angry expression in her eyes became a radiant glow, which came from a heart full of gratitude for the love and blessings she received from her heavenly Father. Her eyes sparkled with a new light.

"I'm so glad you never gave up on me." She tells people how I would just keep preaching to her about God and His love, even when she'd snap at me. "I don't want to hear about your God!" I would stop for then but the next time I'd see her I would eventually work the conversation around to God and His love for her. And I prayed. It really takes boldness to care about whether or not people receive eternal life with Jesus.

A few years back, Julie took a trip to Alaska and met with her aunt who had abused her. "God punished me for all the terrible things I did to you, Julie. I lost a foot to cancer," she confessed.

Julie forgave her. "I could never have forgiven her without the love of God working in me," she insists. After that same aunt's death, Julie made a trip back to Alaska for her funeral. Even the younger generation of Eskimos seemed to have heard the story of how her aunt mistreated her.

"We are so glad you came," they told her.

Now, Julie is glad she's not only a member of her Eskimo heritage, but also a member of God's family and an heiress who will inherit God's heavenly Kingdom.

"I tell you, whoever acknowledges me before men, the Son of Man will also acknowledge him before the angels of God" (Luke 12: 8).

🌸 An Easter to Remember

When we'd started our RV trip about two weeks before Easter, my husband, Kerry, couldn't take five steps without resting. He remained on oxygen most of the time, from the pulmonary fibrosis restricting his lungs. He had recently suffered from a terrible flu and he coughed almost constantly. Before our trip the doctor started him on antibiotics. He arranged to have Kerry pick up oxygen on the way.

Our first stop was close to home, but after about a week we decided to go on to the Rancho Oso Preserve, near Santa Barbara, California. The air was pure and our view breathtaking. Mountains encircled our RV. At the base of the mountains, well within our view, was an operating ranch with horses, goats, cows, one pig, and some chickens.

Instead of leaving for Palm Springs, we extended our stay to include Easter. On Easter morning we arrived at the adult lodge, five minutes before the Easter service scheduled for ten. The parking lot and the lodge were empty. "Do you think we got mixed up, and they're holding the Easter Service at the stone lodge or in the chapel?" I asked Kerry.

"They aren't using the chapel yet because it's not finished, and it's full of building materials. We can check the stone lodge," he replied.

I questioned the manager who was busily working in the kitchen. "Where is the Easter service being held?"

"The minister couldn't make it. If you want an Easter service it will have to be member generated, and it is held at the adult lodge," she answered.

"We'll have a service even if my husband and I are the only ones attending," I told her. "Where are the hymnals?"

She told me where to look in the chapel. Knowing Kerry was too weak to struggle with hymnals, I hurried to the chapel to find them, placing them in two stacks as high as I could carry, and I headed back to our truck.

I found Kerry talking with a woman and a young boy dressed in black slacks and a white dress shirt, ready to go to church. My husband introduced them.

"Adrian decided to come to attend the Easter service instead of going fishing with the rest of the boys," his mother, Christine, told me.

"I'm happy you're here," I told them. "Now there will be at least four of us to worship."

"Why so many hymnals?" Kerry asked.

"I'm hoping enough people come to use all of them."

When we arrived, a group of about twenty adults and several children sat, waiting.

"Did you get lost?" one of the men asked. They thought we were the ones scheduled to hold the service.

"We're members like you, who arrived here for church, but found no pastor present. I spoke to the manager who told me the minister couldn't make it. My husband and I thought we'd start the service. The rest of you can join in as we go along. I picked up some hymnals. It looks as if some of you will have to share your hymnal," I said as I handed them out.

Kerry opened with a prayer, and read the Easter story from Matthew, chapter twenty-eight. His voice was loud and clear. I was amazed because usually I could barely hear him.

"We're here to celebrate the resurrection of Jesus. His rising from the grave proved God's power over death. This tells us that through faith in Jesus, we also have the assurance of our own resurrection. First, to new life in Christ, and after we die, our glorified bodies will be raised to everlasting life in God's presence." Kerry went on to give a wonderful message.

Later in the service Kerry told how nineteen years earlier when our pastor preached an Easter sermon at the fair grounds in San Jose, California, he'd finally understood he could make a commitment to follow Jesus. "During the altar call I walked forward to dedicate my life to Jesus. The following Sunday I was baptized. I'm sure many here would like to share how they came to follow our Lord and Savior, Jesus Christ."

Many of those gathered gave their testimony.

Then a woman volunteered to play the piano. We sang all the hymns they called out. Two of the old favorites, included, "Amazing Grace," and "Jesus Loves Me," for the children. While my husband led the singing, I marveled, because his voice was strong and clear, and he didn't stop to cough even once.

Kerry said a prayer and asked those who wanted to pray for someone or give a praise to God, to add their prayer to his. After many prayed, the service ended with the Lord's Prayer.

"Now this was a wonderful way to worship!" one of the men told us. "In the early days of the church, people just met together in their homes and praised and worshipped God."

"My guess would be their service was very much the same way we worshipped here today. I really enjoyed this service," another guest stated. Others agreed.

Adrian's mother told me how he feared death, so I had a talk with him, letting him know he could live forever in God's presence with a perfect body, if he believed in Jesus and was willing to follow Him. I told Adrian to think about how it would be if he went to sleep at his grandmother's house. After you fell asleep, your mother came in, picked you up, carried you to her car, drove you home, carried you in, and laid you down on your own bed. When you awakened the next morning, you would be safe at home.

"When you die it is just like going to sleep at your grandmother's house and your heavenly Father picks you up and carries you to your heavenly home; and when you awaken the next morning you are safe in the home your Father in heaven prepared for you. Perhaps your grandmother or grandfather, or one of your friends, or even one of your parents will be there to meet you, if they too had died believing in Jesus. You would know you were home, but it would be your heavenly home and there's no place safer than being with Jesus."

After our discussion, Adrian asked questions until he seemed completely satisfied. He left to find his mother who had been talking with Kerry. We drove Christine and Adrian to their RV.

When we returned to our RV, where I had several copies of my children's book, *Matthew's Journey into the Deep,* I found one and wrote a message and signed it. I'd written, "Adrian, I hope you'll always remember Easter Sunday 1997." I hurried back to their campsite and handed him the book just as they were leaving.

Christine got out of their car and came over to hug me. "You don't know how much you and Kerry helped Adrian today. I don't know how to thank you. I just thank God that you both were here today."

"I got all the thanks I needed when I heard Kerry speak so loud and clear, and hearing him sing with that wonderful voice again brought tears to my eyes. He could never have done it without God's strength. He never coughed even once. He's been so sick, and it's been a long time since he's been able to talk and sing like that without coughing. Christine, you can't imagine the joy that filled my heart. I think it gave Kerry real joy, to be able to do that." Christine and I hugged again. We knew this day was special!

"This day is sacred to the Lord your God.... for the joy of the Lord is your strength" (Nehemiah 8:9b,10b).

A special night out for Kerry and Gwen.

15

Secure in Jesus

*And just as we have borne the likeness of the
earthly man* [Adam], *so shall we bear the likeness of the Man from heaven* [Jesus]
(1 Corinthians 15:49).

- "God Sent You"

- By Divine Appointment

- God's Unfailing Love

- A New Life Begins

- From Peace to the Valley of Grief and Back

- Loved, Wanted, and Used by God

*No eye has seen, no ear has heard, no mind has con-
ceived what God has prepared for those who love him—
but God has revealed it to us by his Spirit.... We speak,
not in words taught us by human wisdom but in words
taught by the Spirit* [of God] (1 Corinthians 2:9-10,13a).

185

❀ "God Sent You"

Numerous times people have told me, "God sent you to me." It amazes me every time I hear it.

Janet was one of those people. In Lithia Park in Ashland, Oregon, we sat on a bench and talked. I had questions to ask Janet, because she'd once lived in Ashland, and I wanted to write a travel piece about this town known for its Shakespearean theater. I told Janet that I'd left my husband sitting by the duck pond, because he didn't have enough breath to walk on farther with me.

Janet told me she had Parkinson's disease, and she was in Ashland to see her doctor who had just recently made the diagnosis. She held up her hand, showing it had a slight tremor.

"How fortunate you are that the doctor found out so early," I remarked. I told her about how we traveled much of the time, even though my husband had cancer and pulmonary fibrosis. "This is our fourth trip this year, and we are planning another one to go see our daughter in Virginia, at Christmas time. We'll travel as long as God gives us the strength. We've found out it will all work for our good if we just trust Him. I've learned to thank God even for those things I don't like."

"What you're telling me is what I needed to hear," Janet told me. "God sent you to me today. Thank your husband for giving me this time to spend with you."

It had been easy to talk with Janet about my faith in God and how He allows everything that happens to us for a reason. I had the most wonderful sense of fulfillment when we said our goodbyes.

I felt happy that God sends me to help others.

The next day, my husband said he was going to Medford and I asked if I could go along. Janet lived there and she'd given me her phone number and address. I wanted to sign one of my books and give it to her. I called Janet, and she said it would be easier for her to meet me at one of the big stores there in Medford.

In Medford we met, and I handed Janet my book with a special message I'd written inside, and we started talking again in the store where we were surrounded by health foods and vats of honey and syrup. Again, we spoke like old friends, and I knew that it was the love of Jesus in each of us which bonded us to one another.

When Kerry caught up with us, she thanked him for relinquishing me the day before so I could talk with her. "God sent your wife to me, you know," she stated.

"Other people have told me that before," my husband told her. "I'm just happy God uses her in this way."

Kerry and I take advantage of every occasion we can to see the beauty of God's creation. Sometimes I know we are led to stop certain places to see someone like Janet, who became my friend in such a short time. I intend to keep in touch and visit her again one day, so we can continue the wonderful fellowship we enjoyed in the Lithia park in Ashland, Oregon, and in Medford, on those two special days.

"As you sent me into the world, I have sent them into the world" (John 17:18; Jesus' praying to our heavenly Father about His disciples).

❀ By Divine Appointment

One Sunday in church, they announced a weekend seminar called "Exchanged Life" for those interested. The cost to attend was one hundred dollars, which could be paid at the end of the service.

I remember thinking, *That's kind of expensive.*

Throughout the rest of the service, I had a definite urging to attend that conference. Remembering how God speaks to me through urging and inner nudges and not wanting to miss any blessing He wanted to give me, I went to where our pastor indicated we could sign up, and I wrote a check for one hundred dollars without even thinking about it. That was strange, because I am very frugal with how I spend my money.

During the week I received a phone call from our church. "There's a woman who goes to another church who wants to attend the "Exchanged Life" Conference, and she has no way to get there. Since you are attending, could you pick her up and take her home afterward?" I was asked.

"Sure, I can do that." I was always ready to help someone to get to worthwhile seminars or conferences. I took her address and got the directions to her home.

The woman's name was Marsha and she was nice company. We attended the whole weekend conference, and then on the way home we got into a conversation regarding a subject I felt passionately about. I spoke very vehemently about this issue because I felt quite strongly about what God's stand was. After I finished giving my opinion according to what I felt the Bible taught, I looked over at Marsha. She was crying.

I felt awful. I pulled the car over and parked so I could find out what I'd done. "Marsha, I'm sorry if I said something that hurt your feelings. Please forgive me."

"You think you've just been talking to me, but what you've told me was an answer from God. He sent you to talk to me and show me His will. I'm crying because it touches my heart to know God cares about me enough to send someone personally to answer the questions I've been asking Him in my prayers."

I was stunned by what Marsha told me, but happy to know why God had urged me to go to this conference I hadn't planned to attend. I praised God for using me for His purpose and I prayed He would use me again.

Since His answer was for Marsha's ears, perhaps it wasn't meant for others. I don't know. I only know I fulfilled my heavenly Father's will without even being aware of it at the time.

"...Whoever wants to become great among you must be your servant... just as the Son of Man did not come to be served, but to serve, and to give his life a ransom for many" (Matthew 20:26,28).

God's Unfailing Love

"I know God loves me because he sent you to tell me about Him," my husband, Kerry, told me during the year before he died. He continued, "God is so good to me—so merciful and kind. He's been gracious and generous, giving me so much to be thankful for. He gave me you!" The power of God's grace and love were present in my husband's praise.

Kerry was fighting a second type of cancer. This time it was the faster growing prostate cancer and his lung walls were filling with another fatal disease—pulmonary fibrosis. He never complained about the hand God dealt Him. Rather, He praised God constantly. Kerry had a remarkable attitude up until the last six months of his life, when less and less oxygen got to his brain. Even then his words expressed the joy of God's Spirit at work in him. God loves our sacrifice of praise.

Many people in Kerry's condition would have moaned about their lot in life just knowing they had two fatal diseases. Meanwhile, we were still traveling abroad. We both had the faith that he'd make the trips all right, and he did.

Earlier, while Kerry still had enough breath, he'd spend each Wednesday morning on the golf course playing golf (riding, not walking). Twice a week he went to the fitness gym to work out and expand his lung power. Instead of focusing on his lack of lung power, he focused on keeping what he had, and praised God for what he could do. On Tuesday evenings, he shared God's love with a few men from church who came to our home to discuss what God was doing in their lives. Generally he was comforting them.

Years Pass Still
World Travellers, 1996

When Kerry retired at sixty, he told me, "If I don't retire now we'll never get to travel." It had become a struggle for him to keep going until sixty, because cancer was already at work in his body. We started out on a trip around the United States the day after he retired. We'd purchased a GMC truck and fifth wheel for only $15,000, and we used it ten years quite extensively. It was worth our flying over to Arizona and driving it back. We'd traveled around this country in two smaller campers. The first one we used right after we were married, and then we got a little larger one and finally the fifth wheel. We enjoyed Canada and the United States in our campers, and before he retired, we'd already started taking cruises on his vacations.

Everyone always asked us what our favorite trip was. We agreed that our favorite trip of all times was a cruise that started out in Canada, went to Hawaii, Western Samoa, Tonga, and to a number of stops in New Zealand. Probably the most spectacular sight was cruising down Milford Sound and back again with huge snow-capped mountains jutting out of the water almost close enough to touch. It was a glorious sunny day, and the photographs were marvelous. The scene changed every few moments, and the proximity of those huge mountains, covered in snow with the sun shining on them, took our breath away. Our pictures showed people standing looking up at that awesome sight, with their mouths opened in awe, with snow so close it seemed they could almost have licked it like a snow cone.

Another beautiful sight was the abundance of flowers blooming in the gardens of Christchurch, New Zealand. First they made lovely photo shots and later I painted some water color pictures of those lovely scenes. It was our fall and New Zealand's spring. It seemed odd to see cows grazing right on the hills in the middle of Auckland. They weren't even fenced.

There could be no more hospitable people in the world than those in New Zealand. For example: I needed enough paper to wrap my daughter, Terry's, birthday present, and the clerk cut a piece of large paper in half, saying, "You won't need the whole piece," and charged me half the price. She pulled off enough tape to do the small package and just enough ribbon and charged me a few cents. I was amazed.

Sidney, Australia, our next stop, has to be one of the most beautiful ports in the world because of its famous opera house and bridge. The whole city is spectacular and the stores very quaint. Australians are trying hard to get a reputation for being hospitable like the New Zealanders, and they are kind and helpful as well. After Sidney, we explored Adelaide and Melbourne, and then we traveled to Tasmania.

This is where the Tasmanian Devils live. We were told this was the only place they can stay alive. When you first see them they look like cuddly little bears, with sort of long tails, and I wondered where on earth cartoonists got the idea to picture them as they do. When they opened their mouths, I saw the jagged teeth pictured in cartoons.

When the food came out, we watched them turn into little monsters. They snarled, showing their jagged teeth. They bit each other, trying to prevent others from getting food. I have never seen an animal anywhere with such a terrible disposition.

From Tasmania we traveled to Bora Bora, one of the most unique places in all of our travels, and then on to Tahiti, which was a little more commercial than I expected. However, we rode out in the country and saw a refreshing waterfall, flowering plants, and an enormous turtle. Then on to Fiji, and next to the Hebrides Islands, the hottest spot in our sixty-two day cruise. Even there the temperature was in the low nineties; it wasn't cold anywhere. Our cruise ended in Los Angeles, California. Everyone who took that trip said it was absolutely the most wonderful cruise they'd taken. During the sixty-two days, I can't remember one day of bad weather in all that time.

Each morning, we had Bible class aboard ship. We loved the pastor and his wife, who took the whole trip so they could provide religious services and Bible Study for those who wanted it. After Bible Study we had our exercise classes. By then we were ready to eat the kind of breakfast they serve. I actually lost weight, even though I ate everything I wanted. By exercising and walking the deck a number of times daily, the food didn't add inches or put on pounds. Kerry and I received two jackets each from the points we made doing shipboard workouts and walks. They awarded the points for eating healthy food and taking part in exercising and walking activities. After this cruise, Kerry's cancer test had gone into the safe zone. Later it raised again.

Kerry and I came from poor families and that made this wonderful cruise seem even better. We met a new friend, Dorothy, on that cruise and she visited Kerry and me in San Jose. We took her on one of Kerry's last trips to show her Carmel by the Sea. She still writes and calls me, and we have a cruise planned for April this year.

My memories from trips are breathtaking. Some mornings I awaken in Madeira, Portugal, where they have the most beautiful tile sidewalks and streets and brilliant colored flowers for sale everywhere. In daydreams I think about Madrid, Spain, where the people are still out milling on the street at midnight. People are so lively in Spain, appearing more energetic than people anywhere else in the world. They must shop rather than watch television, because so many Spaniards are on the street at midnight. We covered a lot of ground in Spain. I loved Toledo because of the history of five different religions living together in harmony in that one small city. One of our guides told us that is where the expression, "Holy Toledo," originated. In Missouri, that was one of my favorite expressions. I had no idea it came from a real town in Spain that I would one day visit.

St. Petersburg, Russia, is another spot I'll never forget. There is so much beauty there, and the Pavlovsk Castle outside of St. Petersburg intrigued me. The part we visited didn't seem overdone or extremely elaborate like many other castles, but it was beautifully furnished. Actually it consisted of eight sections, comprising 306 rooms.

The skies were so blue with fluffy white clouds the day we visited, our pictures looked like we had a fake back drop. The architecture was so grand and the art work so exquisite in St. Petersburg, it did not resemble the Russia I had always pictured in my mind. The Winter Palace is built in the lavish style of Russian baroque. The one room I will never forget is the Malachite Room of the Winter Palace. It has eight columns, two fireplaces, lamps, vases, and tables decorated with malachite and shining gold, a striking and unusual combination.

One cannot travel to St. Petersburg without visiting the Hermitage Pavilion with its park and numerous fountains. Inside the Hermitage are exhibits from royal palaces and private collections numbering more than fifteen thousand. It boasts twelve thousand sculptures and in total over two million exhibits. One section contains a vase collection, carved stone, jewelry, and a rare collection of Roman portraits and Greek sculpture. It would have taken weeks, or maybe months, to view all the works of art displayed there. I admit, I wasn't prepared for all the beauty I found in St. Petersburg.

The Russian food was very different from ours. They served us a banquet. First we had all types of cheeses and fish and salads, and we thought that was all there would be, and then they seated us and served borsch on white linen tablecloths. I loved it. I think I had three bowls full. The meat served during our main course had an inlay of darker meat cut in a design within a lighter meat on the outside. It tasted good.

Everyone at our table had a small plate of orange caviar they didn't want. Kerry did, so he had six or seven small extra plates of caviar that he spread on crackers. He knew he wouldn't have another opportunity like that again. The desert looked like a combination of jello and ice cream. A few sour red berries, smaller than cranberries, were drizzled over the top. I enjoyed it all and everything was so different than I eat at home, I did not get sick. They had set a glass of vodka by each place. We all thought it was water and took quite a swallow. It was tasty. I took some sips during dinner, though I don't drink at home. I must admit, their vodka was a whole lot better than ours.

While we ate, dancers performed. Changing their costumes quite frequently, they were a delight to watch. We left Russia happy, never feeling under surveillance as I've heard other visitors state. I doubt the rest of Russia is as grand as St. Petersburg.

The rich and the famous on earth have had no more wonderful adventures than Kerry and I experienced. When we love God, He gives us the desires of our hearts. Kerry and I wanted to travel, and first God brought the two of us together and then He made it possible for us to travel. Every time I put the down payment on a trip, I trusted that the rest would be available when it needed to be paid, and it always was. We never skimped on our donations to save for a trip, but the money was always accessible.

Wanted by God

Our doctor, David Sobel, the head of education in a number of Kaiser Hospitals, expressed how proud he was to know Kerry and me and how we handled Kerry's serious illnesses and dealt with my health problems as well. He told me, "You need to write how you and Kerry traveled and enjoyed life in spite of such serious illness. You're doing what every couple needs to do, but most do just the opposite when they're ill. You're enjoying life instead of staying at home to be close to your doctor and hospital. You are to be commended for your courage."

We both simply trusted God and He never failed us. I figured if one of us died, we would die happy doing what we loved to do.

Once I asked Kerry what he would say if someone asked him how he had the courage to keep traveling, and this was his answer:

"I'm used to getting short of breath. I know God is able to sustain me however He wants me to be. He'll provide us with His strength to get us where we're going. Whenever our truck or fifth wheel broke down, or our health has been threatened while traveling, God has directed us to whatever we needed without much problem. God provides His wisdom so we make the right decisions. His grace and love are always available when we ask for His help. We continue to travel and we praise Him for giving us this opportunity."

On our first trip around the United States, we tried to make it in three months and that rushed us too much. So on our second trip we allowed four months. There is so much to see in this beautiful country. I had no idea how magnificent Niagara Falls could be both from the Canadian side and from New York. The falls are powerful and beautiful. Oak Creek Canyon and Sedona, Arizona, come to my mind as beautiful areas that all Americans would enjoy. Bryce Canyon, Capitol Reef, Arches National Park, and Monument Valley in Utah are all photographers dreams.

I love to visit the Colorado National Monument near Grand Junction. Everyone should ride the forty-five miles of railroad between the two old mining towns of Durango and Silverton. The views and mountain scenery are spectacular. Ouray Colorado, called the little Switzerland of America, is another spot I remember with fond memories, as well as Aspen, Vail, and Glenwood Springs, which boasts the largest outdoor mineral springs swimming pool. Pennsylvania has lush pastoral landscapes, and Lancaster County is an area we enjoyed tremendously. Another state with dairy farms is Wisconsin. The Wisconsin river carved a beautiful gorge through sandstone, forming the Wisconsin Dells. They can be seen by a boat ride through the dells. I found the hill country in Texas to be a beautiful area in that region. The Carlsbad Caverns in New Mexico are the largest and most spectacular of all the caves we encountered in our travels.

In California there are the Redwoods, the beautiful beaches, and the Santa Cruz mountains, all within a few miles of each other. Monterey and lovely Carmel are places I love to visit. Mendocino, off the beaten path, is another quaint town, as is Sausalito on the other side of the Golden Gate Bridge. Hearst Castle at San Simeon is a reminder of past wealth. It is furnished with artistry from around the world and is lavish to behold. Everyone loves Big Sur, not far from Hearst Castle. Point Reyes is located north of the picturesque city of San Francisco. Both are places to visit. However, San Francisco is chilly in the summer. May is a good month to see San Francisco, as is the fall, if you want to miss the colder summer months. When it is hot inland, San Francisco is cold and foggy.

Yosemite National Park is a place filled with breathtaking scenery. A drive up the coast of California and Oregon is something you won't forget. We stopped to take a ride on the shifting Oregon Dunes. It's quite a thrill. In Ashland Oregon, Lithia Park is one of the most beautiful parks where I love to visit any time of the year. This town has a live theater year round, and we enjoyed taking in a play or two each time we visited.

That brings us to the state of Washington. Olympic National Park and the rainforest were wonderful to see. I had seen the Ranier National Park before. Both are well worth seeing. In Wyoming, Yellowstone National Park is full of geysers, including Old Faithful, bubbling mud volcanoes, and plunging waterfalls. Grand Tetons is Wyoming's other National Park, known for its abundance of wildlife. Devil's Tower National Monument is also in this state, nicknamed "The Cowboy State."

We enjoyed North Dakota and especially the Theodore Roosevelt National Park just outside of Medora. South Dakota has the black hills and the badlands, but the sculptures of George Washington, Thomas Jefferson, Theodore Roosevelt, and Abraham Lincoln immortalized in stone on Mount Rushmore, are the main attractions.

Each state has beautiful spots. I've only touched on a few things we enjoyed about our wonderful country. My mind is being flooded with other states we love, but I'd like to tell you about some of the cruises, too.

In 1996 we sailed around the Cape of Norway, traveling between the fjords where the Vikings lived. The grandeur of the spectacular waterfalls, the magnificent mountains, and the surrounding beauty were awesome. Later that same year we cruised to South America and traveled from Peru to Chile, to Argentina, to the southern most city called Ushuaia. We crossed through the Andes mountains by bus. What a breathtaking view! We cruised around Cape Horn and we stopped at the Falkland Islands. Next, we visited Uruguay, a prosperous looking country.

We flew home from Rio de Janeiro, where we saw the statue of Jesus on top of the highest mountain. At night, with His statue completely lighted, it looked as if Jesus was beckoning the people to come to Him because of His outstretched arms.

In 1997 we finally got to see Switzerland, the one place I'd wanted to visit ever since I was a child. We treated our eldest daughter, Terry, and her husband, Wally, to this trip for their thirtieth wedding anniversary. We made use of Wally's strength, allowing him to carry Kerry's oxygen. We took a tour of all the major cities in Switzerland by bus, and we drove into and out of Italy where we enjoyed some of Italy's magnificent lakes, including the Lake Como.

We had the pleasure of cruising down the Rhine, seeing picturesque places like Heidelberg, Germany, and Strasbourg, France. The impeccably kept vineyards of Switzerland were one of the most astounding sights of the trip. They displayed perfection in their planting and their care. Not one weed could be seen in the gardens and vineyards of Switzerland. They were works of art. Switzerland is a gorgeous place.

When we first arrived in Zurich, Switzerland, it was raining. I started praying at once for sunshine to better see the countryside and especially traveling down the Rhine. God smiled down sunshine on us throughout our stay and, according to the residents of Switzerland, the first sun they'd seen that year was the day after we arrived. The sunshine all the way down the Rhine made our trip more enjoyable. I was able to snap lovely pictures of the castles, vineyards, and the picturesque countryside. We were so happy we had taken this last chance to travel in Switzerland. God has certainly revealed Himself in the beautiful creation of this marvelous world.

Soon after we arrived home we got a call that our brother-in-law, Bill, had died. We immediately packed and flew back to be with Kerry's sister, Barb, and the rest of his family in St. Paul, Minnesota. We took a short trip with Barb up to the great lakes.

After we returned home, Kerry still wanted to go to the Olympic National Park in Washington State. We headed out with our fifth wheel for a trip to Washington and Canada in 1997 after flying back from Minnesota. We spent time in the Olympic Park and took wonderful photos in the rain forest with the sun shining. Afterward, we went into Canada. We were fortunate to be asked to join Phil and Ingrid Shelton for their Thanksgiving dinner in Abbotsford, Canada. She's a writer I got to know at a Writer's Conference. They told us about the Mitner Gardens not far from their home, which rivaled the beauty of the Butchart Gardens we had already visited for the fourth time.

We came back to San Jose, where we learned my brother Henry was spending Thanksgiving in Coarsegold, California, visiting he and his wife's family. Henry lived in Hawaii and we hadn't seen him since we'd gone there before Kerry's colon cancer operation. We had a wonderful visit, and since our Thanksgiving is later than Canada's, we were treated once again to a terrific Thanksgiving feast with turkey and ham. It was fortunate we made that trip since my brother died before they could return to Hawaii, less than two weeks after our visit with him. I'm so happy I had that time with him. He looked healthy and no one would have guessed he would be heaven bound in less than two weeks.

Our fifth and last trip in 1997 was back to see our daughter, Terry, her husband, Wally, and our two granddaughters in Alexandria, Virginia, for Christmas. All these trips were the year before Kerry died. He wanted to crowd in all the traveling he could.

Our trips in 1998 were to take Kerry's sister, Sandi, and our Chicago friend, Dorothy, to Carmel By the Sea. Our last trip was to take our RV and set it up under a huge tree in San Benito, California. Squirrels and bunnies scurried about, redheaded woodpeckers pecked on RV windows because they could see the reflection of the tree limbs in the windows. Three of our grandchildren, Adam, Amberly, and Sarah accompanied us. They loved playing with toads and frogs by the stream and kept bringing their latest catch for us to see. These are the three grandchildren we took to Sunday School from the time they were two. They also attended my backyard Bible Clubs. They all believe in Jesus. I have never seen children so filled with joy.

I often talk to them about the invisible world beyond this one where we will live one day. By faith we all know it exists. When belief in God and His Son, Jesus, has been acknowledged, God's Holy Spirit enlightens our minds in spiritual matters. I pray I will always be able to communicate God's remarkable joy and His unfailing love in this world and the next!

The Lord delights in those who fear him, who put their hope in his unfailing love (Psalm 147:11).

🌼 A New Life Begins

Dr. Newman looked me straight in the eye and said, "Personally, I don't think your husband will make it through the night. Therefore, I'm allowing you to spend the night in his room."

Up to this moment, Kerry had been doing quite well. He'd had his ups and downs, but just two weeks earlier he'd ridden his scooter about two miles to Denny's where we'd attended a late morning breakfast with a group from our church. It seemed impossible he could be this much worse. Last night he'd started vomiting a black liquid, which the doctors had now identified as old blood. I'd been up with Kerry most of the night, and the next morning he was still vomiting. The first nurse I'd talked to at our HMO was no help at all.

"Well, it's not as if your husband's doctor is right here. I really don't know what you expect me to do."

"Please put someone on the phone who will know what to do," I insisted. The next nurse, older and more experienced, came on the phone and asked to speak with Kerry. When she heard how he strained to even speak, she told me to call 911.

In minutes, there was pounding on the front door. I opened it and eight people rushed by me. One climbed on Kerry's bed. One bent over him, one stood in back of him, another stood in front of him, and their questions sounded like rapid gunfire.

He was jostled over on the stretcher with all eight people hovering over and around him. He was carried to one of the emergency units, then hoisted up and slid into the ambulance. Kerry waved to the alarmed neighbors who watched the emergency vehicles zoom off with their lights flashing and sirens wailing. I filled them in on what had happened.

A few minutes later, one of the emergency vehicles came back around the block and the driver motioned me over. "I wanted to let you know that the emergency room here at Santa Teresa is full. They are taking your husband to the emergency room in Santa Clara."

"I don't have the slightest idea where that hospital is," I told the paramedic. He gave me some hurried instructions and then pulled out to answer another call. I learned to get there the long way around.

Three evenings later, Dave, our neighbor from across the street made his way over to Santa Clara to visit Kerry. He shared what Kerry's friendship and counseling had meant to him. "I don't see how I'll get along without you, Kerry. You're the only one who has shown empathy toward my situation."

I hadn't realized they'd become such close friends. He stopped by when I was at the gym working out, or shopping for groceries. Dave announced he'd like to sing for Kerry, and we were delighted, especially when we heard his beautiful pure voice singing right on key. He sang every gospel song he could think of over a three hour period.

He told us his car had been diagnosed with a broken head gasket, but God had let him know He wanted him to visit Kerry that night. He knew he might be making things worse by driving the car the way it was, but as it turned out later, he didn't have a broken head gasket after all and it was comparatively inexpensive to repair. If Dave had waited until the next day, Kerry wouldn't have heard any of Dave's beautiful singing

"Peace, peace, wonderful peace," he started another beautiful hymn. I felt completely at peace, even though I knew Kerry would be leaving this earth very soon for his heavenly home. One song followed after another. The beautiful melodies, showing an expression of Dave's love for us, filled the room. I didn't want him to stop singing, but it came time for visitors to leave. Kerry thanked Dave for sharing his gifted voice with us, and soon after he left, Kerry was sound asleep. I decided to go home and try to get a little sleep, too. Driving home I thought about what Kerry had told me earlier that day.

"David (his son) has got our house in Soquel almost remodeled. I'm sorry that you'll have to move down there without me." It had always been my dream to retire in Soquel, just outside of Santa Cruz. I'd been renting that extra home for thirty-six years. "I'm sorry I won't get to help you move, but God seems to have other plans for me," Kerry had told me.

I had assured Kerry that I'd make it fine, as long as I relied on God's strength to see me through. When I arrived home there were nineteen calls I needed to answer. I called a number of them and finally got into bed very late. I had hardly slid into bed when the phone rang. It was Kerry's doctor. "Your husband is getting very low. You'd better get here as soon as possible. He's still alive but he won't last long."

When I was told to get there fast, I panicked and decided to take the quicker route I hadn't tried before. I knew I'd made the wrong turn a minute after I'd done it, but there was nowhere to turn around until I'd traveled almost to the airport, which was miles away from Santa Clara. Trying to find some streets I knew, I ended up doing U-turns in unlikely places. One street name sounded familiar and I took it. No wonder I recognized Market Street—I'd bought all my carpets from a store on that street. I was surprised but happy to see it opened so early in the morning. I dashed inside.

"Is there any easy way for me to get to 280 going north?" I asked.

"Just go to the next corner and turn right and that will lead you right to 280 north."

"Oh, thank you," I called out as I sprinted out the door. "Thank You, Lord, for leading me to ask. Maybe I'll still make it in time. Lord, please keep Kerry alive until I get there," I pleaded.

After a number of wrong turns I arrived at the hospital and rushed into Kerry's room. He was in a deep sleep just like he'd been the day before. His breathing had slowed; however, it seemed more erratic, even though the oxygen was pushed as high as it would go.

"Kerry, Kerry. Wake up and talk to me! Please look at me. I love you, honey. I want to tell you goodbye." I rubbed his thin bony arms and his once sturdy legs, all the time pleading with him to acknowledge I was there. I kissed his face and brushed back his hair. "Darling, please speak to me." I remembered how my grandfather had brought my grandmother back in much the same way. I kept hoping I hadn't arrived too late. He was detached, as if in a different world.

Quite suddenly his eyes opened and he looked up. "Darling, I love you so much," I told him. He showed no recognition that I was there. Without even knowing what I was going to say next, I blurted, "Kerry, have you seen heaven yet?"

He heard me. A smile spread across his face and his sparkling blue eyes looked at me. They twinkled with great joy and our spirits united while we silently rejoiced together. I knew he'd seen me and he'd heard my question about heaven. It seemed to bring him back. Then with great effort from way down deep inside of him, came Kerry's answer to my question: "Y-e-a-h." His smile said it all.

I became filled with the most ecstatic joy. I could barely contain my feelings. I wanted to call out so everyone in the hospital could hear. "Did you hear what he said? My darling has seen heaven and he knows he's going home. He's happy and at peace."

I had seen hope and joy mirrored in my beloved's eyes. He wasn't afraid, though death was very near. I was elated because our spirits had made contact and seeing his wide smile and his twinkling eyes was more than I had ever hoped for. When he fell back into his deep sleep, I rejoiced knowing that he had recognized me and that he had, with great effort, answered my question. I felt certain my darling would return to be with his heavenly Father. I could let him go now without any problem.

God's glory had been reflected in his smile and in the mirror of his soul, his twinkling blue eyes. God had answered my prayer, and I was determined never to complain about his leaving ahead of me for the best trip of all. I was filled with joy. I became more sure than ever that there is new life after death for those who love and trust in Jesus.

Kerry had gone home to be with Jesus just like he'd told his daughter, De De, he wanted to do. He'd gone without suffering or lingering in bed for a long period of time. For those blessings I praised my heavenly Father, His Son, Jesus, and the Holy Spirit, who had enabled Kerry to believe in the truth of the written Word. I thanked God for using me as the instrument to awaken Kerry's belief. I knew that God had given Kerry and me new life in Christ that was a vast improvement from the old carnal life we once had known here on earth.

However, I know that when my body dies, my soul will continue in a new spiritual life in God's Presence in heaven. Kerry will be there, not as my husband, but our spiritual oneness with God will be beyond anything we ever dreamed of in this life, and it will be well worth the wait.

When the perishable has been clothed with the imperishable, and the mortal with immortality, then the saying that is written will come true: "Death has been swallowed up in victory."... Thanks be to God! He gives us the victory through our Lord Jesus Christ (1 Corinthians 15:54,57).

❀ From Peace to the Valley of Grief and Back

Kerry had seen a glimpse of heaven. The radiance shining from his face and his affirmative answer which he struggled with great difficulty to utter, assured me that he'd been allowed a preview of what was to come. Those few precious moments remained with me, giving me peace throughout the funeral service and my trip back to Virginia, to my daughter, Terry's, home for Christmas.

I was still filled with peace and joy when I returned home. I actually cheered others who expressed sadness at Kerry's passing. The same joy inspired me throughout the months that followed, while I sold our house in San Jose and made my move to the Santa Cruz area where I became nestled in the village of Soquel surrounded by friends.

God had provided so many wonderful moments in Kerry's and my life together, much more than I'd dreamed possible. I had those moments to recall whenever I felt lonely. During the months following his death, my friends told me numerous times, "You need to grieve." *How could I grieve when I had so much to be thankful for?*

At a concert on the beach, I shed a few tears when they played the songs Kerry and I had danced to. Little things triggered moments of sadness, which were quickly dissipated when I recalled that God took Kerry home in the manner we had both wanted. I would praise and thank God for preparing Kerry for the prospect of entering His heavenly Father's home, and I continually praised God for Kerry's passing without pain.

Several weeks before the year anniversary of Kerry's death, I became quite sick with a temperature, hurting ears, a sore throat, plugged sinuses, a hacking cough, and an aching back. I went to my doctor who said I had an inner ear infection in both ears and in my sinuses. She placed me on an antibiotic.

I slowly felt better. However, when I went in for my check up, my doctor came in to administer a flu shot. Before I knew what she was doing, the needle was in my arm. Four days later I had a full blown attack of the same type of flu I had thought was over. I saw another doctor who returned me to antibiotics. Later, I experienced the most horrific pain when my eardrum burst.

"Oh Lord," I cried out, "I'm seventy and still suffering from broken eardrums. My eardrums have broken now for sixty-six years. Can't You give me a break and let this be the end of broken eardrums?"

Deafness in one ear left me in an almost silent world once again.

After I'd recovered sufficiently, the man who was landscaping my backyard asked me to go to a nursery with him to pick out plants. I saw a plant I loved, and while Al, who was beautifying my yard, went to get something from his truck, I stepped over a string to look at the name on a plant. Just then the nursery sprinkler system burst forth all around me. Wanting to dash quickly out of the spray of water, I slipped, caught the toe of my shoe in the string, and my feet had gone out from under me. I took a terrible fall on my back. Pain pills had helped only briefly and then I had to see an osteopath for treatments. Looking at my back X-ray, I learned from the doctor I had scoliosis, which is a spinal deformity where the spine is shaped like a backward "S". No doctor had ever mentioned this to me and I hadn't noticed it on previous X-rays. The doctor also pointed out osteoarthritis and degeneration of the lower discs.

After the fall, I became very blue and felt sorry for myself. Instead of praising God in the midst of problems as I've advocated, I seemed to be questioning God more the way Job did. When I remembered how forsaken Jesus, God's Only Begotten Son, felt when He hung on that cross because of my sins, separating Him from His Father, I felt ashamed of myself for questioning God, knowing He has a purpose for all things.

God had let me know I was His child, born because He wanted me. That comforted me each time I remembered it, but then after my fall, I could barely walk and even sitting still hurt. *When is all this pain going to stop?* I grieved for my precious Kerry, who always kidded, hugged, and kissed me, helping me fight my distress from pain. He also prayed for me and with me, which always helped.

When I suffer pain, I often ask, "Am I out of Your will, Lord?" On some occasions I have gained new insight of some sin that I haven't admitted and then I implore God to forgive my sin and remove it from me.

Not all pain is from sin, but God allows us to suffer so His glory may be reflected through our sacrifice of praise to Him during our suffering. The easiest way for me to live is to admit that I cannot live in my own strength. I pray for Jesus to live in me and give me His power and strength. When my "old self" is eliminated and my will bows to the authority of Jesus, I can say with Paul, *"I can do everything through Him who gives me strength"* (Philippians 4:13).

In life's trials we have a choice of two ways to respond. We can wallow in self-pity, separated from God, or we can tell Him we need Jesus' Presence more than we need an understanding of why we are in this situation, and then trust God to reveal the reason for our suffering in His good time.

It was December 5th, and Kerry had left this earth on the 7th of December the year before. In two days it would be exactly one year since he'd passed on to his heavenly glory. I was definitely grieving. I didn't know it was possible to miss anyone the way I missed Kerry. I needed his encouragement now in my pain. He'd always lifted me out of despair, making me a better person. His cheerful encouragement and his praying with me several times a day had always helped me get well.

I had no idea that keeping my longstanding dentist's appointment would trigger more pain. The dentist's son, filling in for his father, noticed I had a tooth with an exposed nerve. I knew I did, but I'd learned to live with it. He said he should do a root canal before that tooth gave me terrible pain. I was feeling good that day so I let him do a root canal. Usually after a root canal my pain stops. This time my pain intensified. I called the dentist's number and learned that the one who did the root canal had returned to Sacramento where he lived. I endured a weekend of intense pain.

On Monday, my dental office sent me to a root canal specialist, but he felt the tooth was too hot to disturb and sent me home with a prescription for pain pills that only partially relieved the pain. Finally, I was sent to another root canal specialist. He said, "I'm going to just barely tap your tooth." It hurt so bad I nearly jumped out of the chair.

"You certainly have a live nerve in this tooth," the dentist decided. He spent the next hour and a half doing a second root canal. Again I was placed on antibiotics and sent home. Later, another back molar flared while they worked on my teeth, and that molar had three roots. So, I had to have three root canals before the pain stopped. It took still another round of antibiotics before the problems with my teeth ended.

There had been days that I felt God had forgotten all about me, but then He'd show me He was still answering my prayers in other areas. The marriage of my step-son, Matt, to a wonderful Christian girl, was certainly an answer to prayer. In the Bible I read, *Give thanks in all circumstances, for this is God's will for you in Christ Jesus* (1 Thessalonians 5:18).

I remembered I hadn't been thanking God, and this passage says to thank Him in all circumstances, not just for the good things that happen in life. That passage gave me the answer I needed. I had been complaining instead of thanking God in all circumstances. One thing I know for sure is that God does not like complaining.

I wrote my Christmas letter to our family and friends on December 7th (the anniversary of Kerry's death), telling them of my long period of pain and anguish. I told how my eighteen-year-old grandson, Jai, came for a turkey dinner I'd prepared for him and his father. When he decided to leave, he kept coming back to give me more hugs. My hunger for hugs must have been written on my face. Jai would walk out to the car, turn around, look at me and walk back and hug me again.

He told me, "I'm getting closer to God again." That helped to cheer me, since he was one of the young people who had prayed to receive Jesus during my backyard Bible Clubs. I had really been missing those Backyard Bible Clubs I'd held for so many years. I decided this was the time to prepare for a Bible Club down here.

I needed to be about my Father's business. I decided after making some calls, that August would work the best for most of the kids. I wanted to hear children sing songs about their love for Jesus. I needed to think less about my loss and more about teaching others about how much Jesus loves us.

I climbed out of bed and went to buy gifts for my loved ones, and I wrote checks to send Bibles to prisons and to parts of the world where they were needed. I prayed fervently that God would help me to completely forgive anyone for whom I might hold unforgiveness. I got down on my knees and prayed for all those who needed to be closer to their Lord and Savior, and I thanked God for all of the family members who were seeking Him that they might have victory over sin and death through faith in Jesus. I asked God to please forgive me for complaining and I praised Him for the presence of His Spirit within me.

What peace I experience when I am back living in harmony with God's will.

The day before Christmas I felt much improved and able to travel to visit with four families, who had invited me to their homes over Christmas.

The next morning I packed all the gifts for everyone in my car and headed for Mantica. Julie, my daughter-in-law, invited me for the day before Christmas. She's the wife of Kerry's son, David. Along with their two children, Katie and Kevin, they made my day special. They treated Julie's parents and me to a wonderful dinner. I was overjoyed when Kerry's son, David, offered a beautiful prayer, thanking God, before we ate. At one time David had told his father he didn't even know if he believed there was a God.

Later in the evening, we left Mantica and returned to San Jose, where I spent the night at the home of Julie's parents.

In the morning I called Matt, Kerry's other son, and told him I'd be right over. Matt had recently received Christ into his life, was baptized, and he'd become involved in doing the Lord's work in his church. Starla, a lovely Christian girl, had convinced him he needed God, something Kerry and I had spent years trying to do, with no success.

Wanted by God

Matt is the only person I ever prayed for by lying face-down on the floor to demonstrate my desperation. I pleaded with God to deliver Matt from wrong thinking and wrongdoing and to please call him unto Himself and make him His own. Kerry and I had done all we could do, and at that point, I was relinquishing him to God. Only God could change Matt and we knew it. God answered my prayer, and through the help of a lovely blonde named Starla and a church that truly cared and had patience with him, he learned to do things God's way.

I recently experienced great joy during Matt and Starla's wedding. God worked it all out, bringing two single people and their five children together, who now all love the Lord and each other. It is a beautiful thing seeing how our almighty God works everything to His glory. What a wonderful God we serve. He does hear and answer our prayers.

"God brought Starla into my life the way he brought Dad into yours," Matt told me one of the last times I saw him. I could never describe the joy I feel every time I see or talk to Matt. The other day he told me, "All I want to do now is please God." All praise and honor belong to our faithful Lord.

I'm a blessed woman to have two wonderful step-sons. At one time it seemed quite impossible for me to ever have any sons, but with God all things are possible.

I drove to my daughter, Cindy's, home in Aromas on Christmas afternoon. We exchanged gifts and I was thrilled when Jai said, "My new wallet with the pictures of my family is my favorite gift. I really do have a wonderful family, don't I?" I was pleased even more when Jai asked to say the blessing before our Christmas dinner. I experienced a wonderful holiday filled with the love of God and family.

The next morning I awakened early in order to travel to worship at Twin Lakes Church in Aptos, California. Our pastor, René Schlaepfer, gives a message we can take along with us and put into practice. We are fortunate to have such a gifted pastor.

Although some of our children don't attend church weekly, as I would prefer, I know they have all been called by God.

...God our Savior, who wants all men to be saved and to come to a knowledge of the truth. For there is one God and one mediator between God and men, the man Christ Jesus, who gave himself as a ransom for all men... (1 Timothy 2:3-6).

205

That passage came up recently when I talked with a new friend in the "Comfort Through Christ" class, which is for people suffering from chronic pain. She confided in me that her husband didn't attend church and she couldn't talk to him about her faith because it made him angry. She asked me if I would pray for him to come to know the Lord.

"I'd love to. That's a request that I know is in God's will because God wants all men to be saved." I shared with her, 1 Timothy 2:4. "As for him becoming angry if you talk to him about your faith, don't worry about that. Have the courage to do it anyway." I told her about Julie, who had hated God and got angry every time I told her about the God I knew, and how much Jesus loved her. I also told my new friend that even Kerry had resisted what the booklet on the four spiritual laws said about Jesus being the only way to God. When he came to the page that said, "Jesus is the only way to God," he threw the booklet on the table and said, "Why does it always come to this?"

"A number of people I have witnessed to have become angry before God's Spirit reached them with the truth. I'd back off and wait until another time to bring it up again," I told my new friend. "Never give up."

Walking out of church after the Sunday service, I was surprised to see my new friend walking right beside me. "Oh, Gwen, I have so much to thank you for. My husband and I are finally able to sit and talk to each other. We had the most wonderful discussion this morning, and you're the one who gave me the courage to bring up the subject of my faith to my husband." She threw her arms around me and gave me a big hug.

"That makes me very happy. I've really been praying for you two, and I'm always happy to hear my prayers are being answered. Thanks for telling me."

"You have been such a good example for me because you have so much faith. I'm praying I'll be more like you."

"I think you'd do a lot better praying to be more like Jesus," I said, laughing.

"But God sent you to me. I'm so glad you came to our pain group or I might never have met you. You're like an angel to me."

Those words were music to my ears. Up until that point, I felt maybe I should have stayed in San Jose to keep ministering to the youngsters who used our pool. My new friend's words assured me that I was *wanted by God* right there in my new church. And now I knew why I had suffered so much pain. God wanted me in that "Comfort Through Christ" group for people in pain. Not only did I pray for my friend and her husband, but my prayers were answered. My friend's husband is attending church with her nearly every weekend. Our God is so good!

Our group has become a caring family. We can count on each other. Under God's direction, I am confident this ministry will continue to bring joy into my life and into the lives of all those who attend.

> *I love those who love me, and those who seek me find me.... For whoever finds me finds life...* (Proverbs 8:17,35a).

> *We have not received the spirit of the world but the Spirit who is from God, that we may understand what God has freely given us. This is what we speak, not in words taught us by human wisdom but in words taught by the Spirit, expressing spiritual truths in spiritual words* (1 Corinthians 2:12-13).

❀ Loved, Wanted, and Used by God

While packing to leave for the last lap of the World Cruise at the end of March 2001, I became filled with gratitude toward God for giving me this chance to visit parts of the world I had not yet seen. "Thank You, Lord, for making this trip possible," I prayed. Then God's Spirit prompted me to add: "Lord, while I'm travelling, send me anywhere You want someone to hear the truth about Your great love. Give me the words to say and I'll be your messenger."

I'd taken this cruise seeking the same type of enjoyment I'd had with my husband, Kerry, but it did not happen. I missed sharing the excitement and joy of the exotic ports and the life on the ship with the one I loved. Part of my pleasure had been hearing Kerry's exuberant exclamations about everything he saw, and watching his appetite soar as he ordered the exceptional food on the menu. Listening to his delightful conversation, whether we were alone or with those seated at our table, always endeared him to me.

Without his companionship, I felt like a lost orphan and I mourned his presence more on the cruise than I had at home. I missed the wonderful prayers he'd said at the table for everyone present when we traveled with this same group, except for Kathy's husband, Tiny, who had also died since our last cruise. Kathy agreed cruises weren't as good since Tiny had died. "It's just not the same without him," she told me.

The entertainment had been wonderful on our other cruises and this time it seemed tasteless and dull. Even the food didn't taste nearly as good as when Kerry was beside me. I did, however, enjoy the Bible Classes on the days we weren't on tour. God's Word has always been satisfying to me and when listening to the Word, I didn't feel Kerry's absence.

On Easter morning, April 15th, there were two services. The rabbi, priest, and pastor all took part in the first service held on deck just as the sun started to rise. At nine, every seat in the theater was filled to capacity for an inspiring Easter service, with the Protestant pastor officiating. Hearing voices from around the world singing praises to our risen Lord was an awesome experience.

Since it was a day of rest, that afternoon I went to the top deck to have a leisurely swim and enjoy the beautiful weather. I spent time relaxing in the whirlpool, thinking the heat might help my sore left leg that had been causing me pain for several days. It felt heavy while climbing up to the Parthenon in Athens, Greece, and by the time we arrived in Venice, Italy, I could barely drag my leg to where the gondola ride started.

While in the whirlpool, I noticed my left leg was much larger than my right one. Since my legs are usually slender, it shocked me when I felt how fat the lower part of my left leg felt. Going to my room to get dressed, I saw my friend, Kathy, and mentioned to her how swollen my leg had become.

She looked down at my leg and said, "You'd better get to the doctor. You could have a blood clot in your leg." She recalled another passenger that had a blood clot, and she said his leg looked just like mine.

Blood clot? My ears perked up. My mother died on the doctors' examining table, and there had been a suspicion that a blood clot traveling to her heart may have caused her death. I decided it was time for me to see the ship's doctor.

When I arrived at the doctor's office it was a minute after six. The nurse said, "We're already closed for the evening. Come back in the morning."

The doctor overheard us talking and asked, "What is your problem?" I told him about my swollen leg. He said, "Get up here and let me have a look at it." He measured both legs and the left was definitely larger, red in color and hot. It was extremely painful when he touched the fleshy part of my calf. From the grim look on the doctor's face, I knew he was going to tell me something I didn't really want to hear.

"I want you to stay off of this leg. You have a deep vein thrombosis, which is very dangerous. I'm just thankful I saw you tonight so we can get you to a good hospital in Lisbon, Portugal, tomorrow morning. I don't have the means to take care of you on the ship. I'll give you an injection to start thinning your blood tonight, and tomorrow you must be ready to leave after we dock in the morning." He turned to his nurse to ask her to prepare an injection.

"You'll be taken to your room in a wheelchair. I want you to go straight to bed. Call room service to order your dinner." The phone rang and it was Kathy, calling to see why I hadn't come to dinner. The people at my table were worried about me. The doctor told his nurse to ask Kathy if she and my other friends could pack my bags tonight, so I would be ready to leave the hospital in the morning. She said they'd get me packed.

He turned back to me. "It's fortunate you didn't wait to come see me after we left Lisbon, because there are no more large hospitals on the rest of this cruise that would have given you the care you need." After I'd left the ship, the doctor told Kathy, who is a close friend of his nurse, "If your friend had waited another couple of days, they might have had to carry her off the ship in a body bag." Instead, two husky men carried me in a wheelchair to a waiting car. I suddenly recalled my prayer at home prior to the trip, and I knew in my heart that God had a meeting planned between someone at the British Hospital and me.

Pat, a friend, captured a photo of me being carried from the ship and she caught a smile on my face as I awaited my divine appointment. I felt God was sending me to communicate with someone about His great love. Being His servant always brought joy.

Meanwhile, God was working behind the scenes taking care of every detail. Leslie, one of three Cruise Specialists from Seattle, Washington, was aboard our ship to help any of their clients who might encounter an emergency of some kind. She accompanied me to the hospital and took care of getting me signed in, and presented them with my World Access insurance which completely covered my medical emergency and my trip home. I had no worries about hospital bills.

When I arrived at the British Hospital, Dr. Mario Ferreira, who had been schooled in Boston, was assigned as my primary physician, and he called in Dr. Tieves, a Portuguese cardiologist, when I complained of spasms in my chest. The first EKG showed ischemia, brought on because the thrombosis had produced spasms and temporary angina pain. Dr. Tieves, eighty-two, spoke five languages and was a delight to talk with each time he came to see me. My later EKG's turned out normal.

While in the hospital I thought about all the ports I had managed to see. I'd really seen the main attractions, including Cairo and Alexandria, Egypt;

Istanbul, Kusadasi and Ephesus, Turkey. The ruins in Ephesus were worth taking the trip. Next, Athens, Greece; Venice, Italy, including a gondola ride; and Dubrovnik, Croatia, which was the port I enjoyed most, because four of my friends took this tour, too. I thought it was the most picturesque. We journeyed on to Palermo, Sicily, and Malaga, Spain, before we cruised to Portugal. I saw some of Portugal from the balcony of the hospital, and more on my ride to their grand airport in Lisbon, which was very impressive.

I had a peaceful rest in the hospital, even though I was in a room accommodating three other patients. I talked to a number of people who spoke English. Every day I was constantly on the alert for God's Spirit to show me the one I came to visit. There were actually three people who God encouraged me to speak to about Him. Each time I wondered if I had imparted the message God wanted me to share with that person. I knew God could use my words to accomplish His purpose, so I committed them to Him and asked that my witness be used for His glory.

On Sunday, I tuned in to a Portuguese Catholic mass on TV. Three of us sat up in our beds and enjoyed it. I managed to worship God by reading the priest's lips. I could figure out some of the words I thought he was saying. One patient voiced her disapproval of the service. She sat with her back to the TV, but I noticed when the other patients were reciting prayers or creeds, she joined in saying them along with the other women.

Never have I had better care in a hospital. Dr. Ferriera was very solicitous and extremely thorough. He had explained to me that my blood would have to be thinned for six months to insure that the blood clots were completely dissolved. Meanwhile, I would wear therapeutic stockings and routinely keep my leg elevated. Both he and Dr. Tieves saw me twice a day. A vascular doctor came occasionally.

One patient, a beautiful ninety-eight-year-old Catholic sister, originally born in Ireland, came to Portugal when she was twenty-three and had taught school in Portugal until she was ninety. How eagerly she and I shared the love we had for Jesus and we discussed how tenderly He loves us. We also spoke of the ecstasy we will have spending all eternity with God and our Lord Jesus in heaven. What joy it brought to think of being in God's Presence forevermore. My being in the presence of this Christian saint and sharing with her my vision of our heavenly home, forged a bond between us.

Having had those sweet moments with her every day was better than taking the rest of the cruise. Jesus' love mirrored in Sister Kennedy's eyes allowed me to feel my Lord's Presence in the same way I had His love when my husband, Kerry, looked at me. I had sorely missed seeing Jesus' love reflected in Kerry's eyes since his death, and not seeing that love once on this cruise was the reason I felt so let down.

I hadn't really understood this until I'd seen Jesus' love reflected in the eyes of Sister Kennedy as she shared her love of Him with me. Our mutual love for our Lord bonded us together in spiritual unity and love. My heart was so filled with the joy of the Lord, at times I felt it would burst.

God made me aware that when Jesus' love reflects through our eyes while we share our love for our Savior with others, the person hearing of our love for Jesus may instinctively perceive His love shining through our eyes. This may spark belief in the heart of one who has previously resisted God.

Now I understand better than ever why it is so important for us to ask Jesus to come live His life in and through us. Jesus' love is the love everyone seeks, and His love can radiate through us to others when we give of ourselves unselfishly.

God was showing me how important it is for people to see Jesus' love reflected in the eyes of those who love Him. When I saw Jesus' love mirrored through Sister Kennedy's eyes, who I had never met before, I praised God.

Think how we, who are Christians, could encourage our friends and neighbors by reflecting Jesus' love. I'm sure it happens daily, but not nearly as often as it could. If all Christians mirrored Jesus love what a wonderful world this would be.

I recalled some years ago a woman whose husband had suffered a stroke and she, too, was ill. I had taken her to my doctor for medical care and helped them to get welfare, which they had never needed until tragedy struck. With the help of our pastor we found a warm home they could now afford to rent, and the ladies from our church took turns cooking them hot meals which I delivered to them. One night when I brought their dinner, she looked into my eyes and said, "When I look at you, I see Jesus." I never quite knew what to make of that comment. Now, I wondered if she saw Jesus' love reflected in my eyes, the way I saw His love mirrored in Sister Kennedy's eyes.

After Sister Kennedy left the hospital, I felt anxious to return home. Before I left the hospital, the doctor taught me how to give myself injections to thin my blood. He provided syringes to use on the way home and until I had the chance to see a doctor. He told me that I would need medication to thin my blood for a total of six months to be certain the blood clots had dissolved. Giving myself injections twice a day seemed a little less obnoxious when I considered the insight I had gained on this trip to the hospital.

Dr. Ferreira felt I shouldn't fly home, sitting for sixteen hours straight. He insisted that I take a hotel room in Florida, to rest before the flight across the United States.

God prompted me to ask, "How about a layover in Washington, D.C., where my daughter and her husband could pick me up and take me to their home to rest?" That suggestion became a reality.

Dr. Ferreira requested an ambulance to drive me to the airport in Lisbon, but the insurance company asked, "How about a limousine, instead?"

"I guess that would give Gwen plenty of room to elevate her leg," he answered. "That's the only time I've been asked that question by an insurance company," he told me with a chuckle.

Riding in that luxury Mercedes, I had about a forty minute tour of Lisbon on the ride to the airport. I thought about how God had arranged everything to make my detour to the British Hospital safe, inspiring, and gratifying. I had hoped to serve Him and He had blessed me by fulfilling my longing to see His love reflected in my beloved's eyes. He had shown me His great love by sending His precious servant, Sister Kennedy, so I could see His love mirrored through her eyes. How important it is for us to see God's love reflected in another person's eyes. The people who reflect God's love build up one another and the body of Christ grows stronger.

I glanced out the window of the limousine and saw some of the Lisbon sites I had not seen because I had missed the city tour. I only missed stopping at two islands in the Azores, and the six days crossing the Atlantic ocean, cruising into Florida.

Leaving Lisbon, I flew to Paris where I changed planes and flew into Washington, D.C., where I got to see my daughter, Terry, my son-in-law, Wally, my two granddaughters, Tracy and Tammy, and Tammy's new husband, Tom. It was a wonderful visit provided by my heavenly Father, who plans all things well.

Flying home, I thought about how close I'd come to death. Had the blood clot moved to my heart or brain I would have been in heaven right now. I look forward to heaven constantly, but I knew God wanted me to finish the chronicle of my life.

However, I considered all the people who may read this book and not be certain whether they will spend eternal life with God. The Bible promises eternal life to all who receive Jesus. However, it was our Lord Jesus who said to Nicodemus, "*I tell you the truth, no can see the kingdom of God unless he is born again*" (John 3:3).

When Nicodemus asked how it is possible to be "born again" when we are old, Jesus told him,

> "...*[N]o one can enter the kingdom of God unless he is born of water and the Spirit. Flesh gives birth to flesh, but the Spirit gives birth to spirit. You should not be surprised at my saying, 'You must be born again'*" (John 3:5-6).

A spiritual transformation is needed which takes us out of the kingdom of darkness and places us into the Kingdom of God. I struggled with this passage, "*You must be born again,*" because I knew I had the Spirit of God in me but I had not felt this "new birth." God's Spirit was within me, bringing me slowly to the recognition of the habit of holding on to hurts of the past, which I had started as a very young child . Dwelling on harsh statements, that had been said over and over throughout my life, intruded into my thoughts, preventing God's Spirit from doing His work of regeneration in me. After I prayed for Jesus to come live His life in me, I felt it was Jesus making me aware of my habit of recalling the bad things people had said and done to me. Now I came to an important step in becoming a child of God. I had to acknowledge my sin of unforgiveness toward those who had wronged me.

Our human nature wants to get even, but God tells us to forgive in the way He has forgiven us. He showed us mercy when He allowed His beloved Son to die on the cross for our sins, so it is necessary that we show mercy to those who wrong us, as well.

Oh, the sweet release that comes when we truly forgive another person.

Soon after I had asked for God's forgiveness and had forgiven those who had hurled scathing remarks at me, I started to notice a change taking place. A bud of new life burst forth and finally I blossomed into a new creation. The old had passed away and the new birth had come. Admitting our sin is a difficult thing for human beings. It is so much easier to blame another person for what happened, or even blame God for the way He made us.

The more we try to justify our mistakes, the harder it is for us to forgive others. It may be necessary to ask God to show us where we have offended Him and ask His help in ridding our lives of some certain sin. It is sin that separates us from God, and that is why Jesus, who never committed sin, was the only One who could pay the price with His life's blood as a sacrifice for our sin, because He lived the only life acceptable to God. So, the sinless Son of God became our substitute. God sees us washed clean through the blood of our sacrificial Lamb, His only Son, Jesus Christ.

Our belief in Jesus as our substitute means we recognize we are sinners and that we need a Savior, and that Jesus is the only sacrifice acceptable to God. Since God is holy, there had to be a sufficient mediator to reconcile those who are unholy to His perfect holiness.

Men are opposed to God in their sin and God is opposed to men in His holiness. Since God is opposed to unrighteousness, He will separate from Himself all who sin. He will have no fellowship with the unholy. Unless there is a way of reconciliation, unholy people would have no chance before a holy God. Reconciliation is "making peace" with God, and reconciliation can be accomplished only by Christ, through His blood shed on the cross.

Once you were alienated from God and were enemies in your minds because of your evil behavior. But now he has reconciled you by Christ's physical body through death to present you holy in his sight (Colossians 1:21-22).

Men and women must admit they are sinners and that believing in Jesus is the only way their sins can be washed clean. However, many people still want to decide what will save them, and they can think of many reasons why believing in Jesus is not the way. But Jesus said,

"I am the way and the truth and the life. No one comes to the Father except through me. If you really knew me, you would know my Father as well. From now on, you do know him and you have seen him." Philip said, "Lord, show us the Father and that will be enough for us." Jesus answered: "Don't you know me, Philip, even after I have been among you such a long time? Anyone who has seen me has seen the Father.... Don't you believe that I am in the Father, and that the Father is in me?... [A]t least believe on the evidence of the miracles themselves (John 14:6-11).

We accept man's testimony, but God's testimony is greater because it is the testimony of God, which he has given about his Son.... And this is

the testimony: God has given us eternal life, and this life is in his Son. He who has the Son has life; he who does not have the Son of God does not have life (1 John 5:9,11,12).

Many people have the false notion that they can be good enough and charitable enough to enter heaven on their own merit, but the Bible tells us otherwise:

For it is by grace you have been saved, through faith—and this not from yourselves, it is the gift of God—not by works, so that no one can boast (Ephesians 2:8-9).

Faith is a gift from God and a wonderful blessing. We who have faith can thank God for His remarkable gift. Faith is not a feeling, but it is the assurance that we can trust in the promises of God. The Bible tells us: *Now faith is being sure of what we hope for and certain of what we do not see* (Hebrews 11:1). Spiritual growth comes through exercising our faith. It is faith that enables us to trust God during the painful and fiery trials of life, by not fighting against circumstances we don't like, or turning against God and asking, "Why?" The Holy Spirit show us that God has a reason and He can use even painful circumstances to work for our good and build our faith. The Spirit helps us grow into the people God wants us to become.

When joy bubbles to the surface until we feel we will almost burst, because we know we love God and He loves us and nothing in our lives is more important than that, we have been filled with the Spirit of God. However, since faith is not a feeling or an emotion, there may be times of feeling let down, or maybe not feeling God at all. But He hasn't abandoned us or forgotten who we are, even in long periods of silence from Him. He may be testing our faith to see if we trust Him after we have prayed for Him to come into our lives to direct the path we should take. This is when faith is necessary to keep believing God is a caring God who keeps His promises in His own time (which is not according to our time table) and to wait patiently, knowing He will give us His best.

We all need Jesus because the Bible tells us: *[A]ll have sinned and fall short of the glory of God* (Romans 3:23).

God's solution to our not measuring up or missing the mark, is in John 3:16: *"For God so loved the world that he gave his one and only Son, that whoever believes in him shall not perish but have eternal life"* (John 3:16).

We who are believers know this earth is not our real home, and we look forward to spending eternity with God, first in the present heaven, and later in a new heaven and a new earth God will create. He who overcomes will inherit all of this glorious new world.

I love to picture Jesus walking toward me with His arms outstretched. I see the scarred imprint of the nail in each hand when He wraps his mighty arms around me. Jesus, whispers, "Welcome, my child, I've been waiting for you."

Then I hear the roar of a great multitude of brothers and sisters in Christ, raising their voices singing praises to God for His great love. My voice blends with the voices of those in this great assembly. I am made aware that I have a whole new set of vocal chords from those I now use, part of my new glorified body.

The wedding banquet for the Lamb of God is being prepared for that great day when all believers will be joined to the Groom, who loved us enough to lay down His life, that we might live forever with Him in His glorious Presence.

"Hallelujah!
For the Lord God Almighty reigns.
Let us rejoice and be glad and give him glory!
For the wedding of the Lamb has come,
and his bride has made herself ready.
Fine linen, bright and clean, was given for her to wear."
(Fine linen stands for the righteous acts of the saints.)
Then the angel said to me, "Write: 'Blessed are those who
are invited to the wedding supper of the Lamb!'" (Revelation 19:6-9).

Oh, the joy I felt knowing that I was included in the body of Christ, standing among this great throng, knowing that soon we would become the bride of Christ.

"But when he, the Spirit of truth, comes, he will guide you into all truth. He will not speak on his own; he will speak only what he hears, and he will tell you what is yet to come" (John 16:13).